Have a good read,
Hann
(and join our band :-))

ROCKETS AND REBELS

Monna Nordhagen and Kirsti Rogne

ROCKETS AND REBELS

Strategy for anyone looking to build brands that move people

Introduction by Richard Bonner-Davies

Original title: *Raketter og rebeller*
Copyright original edition © Vigmostad & Bjørke AS 2017
Translated into English by Kirsti Rogne

Copyright © Vigmostad & Bjørke AS 2018
All Rights Reserved

ISBN: 978-82-450-2499-9

Graphic production: John Grieg, Bergen
Typeset by Scandinvian Design Group

Cover design by Scandinvian Design Group
Illustrations: Vegard Aspelund, Oliver Riches
og Truong Vu Pham

Enquiries about this text can be directed to:
Fagbokforlaget
Kanalveien 51
5068 Bergen
Tel.: 55 38 88 00
Fax: 55 38 88 01
email: fagbokforlaget@fagbokforlaget.no
www.fagbokforlaget.no

All rights reserved. No part of this publication may be reproduced, stored in a retrieval system, or transmitted, in any form or by any means, electronic, mechanical, photo-copying, recording, or otherwise, without the prior written permission of the publisher.

Introduction by Richard Bonner-Davies

People running businesses, or heading organizations, consultants, advisers and students all tend to be big readers. We look for inspiration, for best practice and for advice.

We are readers about our competitors and rivals, usually through trade publications and blogs. We also read articles, publications and books, both related to our business or industry, but also to leadership in general.

Our Harvard Business Review reading list is a long one, be that devouring the latest issue, or having our attention drawn to an article from 3 or 4 years ago, that suddenly might prove useful to an issue we are grappling with.

The Economist is, of course, a must-read for most of us in business today, if only to be able to have a point of view on, or to "know enough to be dangerous" about a far-flung conflict or the impact of Bitcoin on today's economy, or the pros and cons of a reduction of the corporate tax rate on society.

And then there are the books we're told we absolutely need to read. Some generalist, like *The best kept secrets of the world's top CEOs* (I think I just made that up but I'm sure it exists), *The 7 habits of highly effective people*, *How to deliver a great TED-like talk*, etc. And some specialist to marketing and marketers, like *Eating the Big Fish*, *Hit Makers*, *Blue Ocean Strategy* and perhaps *Digital Marketing for Dummies*.

This is a big list of "must-reads" considering it comes on top of doing your actual job. Truth is, though, we need this inspiration – to learn from others that have blazed new trails and are happy to share their secrets and failures along the way.

The nagging concern I have when reading much of what I read however, is always one of relevance. What is in this that is useful to me? Books and HBR articles tend to be written by the winners, and as such they are stories delivered through the lens of people who want to demonstrate their success as much as offer you their sage advice and wisdom.

My other source of unease here is that the printed word is discussing something that happened in the past. And let's face it, the world is changing so rapidly, it is tough for any of us to keep up, much less have time to look in the rear-view mirror at what just happened. We now have new ways to talk to our customers, and we make use of new and interactive content to help drive both brand and sales. Rapidly evolving markets, companies, dynamics, channels and challenges keep us all on our toes.

Let's now add to all these challenges; of time (or the lack thereof), of changing dynamics of our markets, our competition and our customers.

What do we tell them? How do we tell them? And when do we tell them what?

In *Rockets and Rebels*, Nordhagen and Rogne have managed to identify the needs of the modern business to answer these questions. They do so in a way that is short-hand to the long reading list; you know, the ever growing, always extensive, never exhaustive list alluded to above. This is at its heart, a compendium of the best and brightest marketing & brand thinking from academics and marketers over the last 50 years, balanced and blended with real-world examples from brands we know and understand.

By doing this, they manage to explain often complex marketing theory in plain English, through the introduction of a brand story, example or anecdote. So, while the book is riddled with theories, models and approaches from the best and brightest marketing minds of the past 30 or so years (like Kotler, Edelman and Morgan), the book is completely up to date in both its thinking and brand examples. Indeed, a somewhat dry subject for many comes alive with anecdotes and examples using brands like Coke, Nike and VisitOSLO.

The chapters are logically laid out and the journey the book takes you on is thoughtful. So, an understanding of your brand's positioning and role is followed by discussions around differentiation, identity and strategy.

But embedded in all of this are some fascinating discussions around things like clearly defining the category in which you operate – and the critical importance of defining this correctly, was for me a real eye-opener.

Nordhagen and Rogne use science and medicine liberally throughout the book, giving you examples of how the human brain works as it considers everything from brand choices to how it engages with stories and storytelling.

This is perhaps then, finally a book on branding and marketing that is accessible, knowledgeable and forward looking, as opposed to ones written about the past. Reading a chapter at a time makes it easy reading - although I admit to reading the whole thing in one sitting.

I can see this book being useful for teams of people, from disparate departments across a company, who are tasked with working together on a major corporate project or merger. Or, for people who want to start a business, large or small, and get their branding right from the start. Or, for young people looking to build the brands of the future. You don't have to be an expert in the field of branding to read this book…but you just might be by the end of it.

London, June 2018

Richard Bonner-Davies

Note from the authors

This book is a true team effort. It has two authors: Monna Nordhagen and Kirsti Rogne. Monna is the main author and the book's narrator.

The writing process has been more or less as follows: Monna writes a twenty page draft, Kirsti cuts it down to ten, adds two, and then rewrites all over again.

We have had long discussions about content, structure, examples, what to include and what not. So many colleagues have helped by offering opinions; alternately boosting our confidence in the project and making sure our feet remained firmly on the ground. Thank you all for that!

We have also learnt a great deal from our clients. While we can't mention you all by name you know who you are.

Our editor, Sven Barlinn, has helped us navigate between the formal requirements of academia and our desire to be as practical as possible.

Not to be forgotten is the creative team responsible for the design of the book. Oli Riches, Vegard Aspelund, Truong Vu Pham, Petter Tangen and Nick Bilmes have sketched, redesigned, and fought for their versions of models, illustrations and layout with superhuman patience throughout the time it took to write this book. We could not be more grateful for, or proud of, the final result.

We are also eternally grateful to our families, in particular Monna's husband Tor and Kirsti's Gunnar, who have suffered through our triumphs and set backs with just the right amounts of support and celebration along the way.

Oslo, June 2018

Monna Nordhagen   Kirsti Rogne

We shape our tools and then our tools shape us.

Father John Culkin

A schoolman's guide to Marshall McLuhan

Table of contents

In the beginning   17
Brand builders need tools too   20
Which tools? And why?   21
The structure of this book   23

Chapter 1
Brands in our time   25
What's happened?   25
Customers are now the most important marketing channels   25
The speed of innovation is higher,
and competition more complex   28
A new role – and a new definition – for brands   30
New times call for new tools   33
SWOTs, value mapping and prototypes   34
The customer decision journey is the new sales funnel   35
From a static to a dynamic strategy paradigm   39
Now, finally, the toolbox   41

POSITIONING
A brand among other things   47

Chapter 2
Category – the door to people's minds   49
Brands according to the brain   50
The King of Category   52
Category properties and brand properties   53
Naming a category   55
Category and the competitive arena   56
Three strategies   57
Deciding what a category is all about   58

Chapter 3
Role   63
Two clear roles – and one other option   63
The market leader   69
The challenger   72
The pioneer   75
What determines a brand's role?   79

Chapter 4
Differentiation – deserving a place in people's mind   83
The differentiation rocket   85
First what, then how   87
Differentiation is a moving target   88
Getting off the ground – the goes-without-saying criteria   89
Towards your destination – differentiating criteria   93
Touchdown – where your brand is unique   95
Differentiation and role   97
Working the differentiation rocket   99
Rocket in action   103

IDENTITY
Branding, its origins and tasks — 108

Chapter 5
Archetypes — 113
Archetypes help brands build relationships — 114
What is an archetype? — 117
What archetypes represent — 118
To make it just a little more tricky – but also more useful — 122
And just one more thing … — 124
Making use of archetypes in your brand building — 125
Off to a good start — 128
A short introduction to the 12 archetypes — 129

Chapter 6
The identity prism — 179
Communication — 181
The brand identity prism structure — 183
Process — 193
Everyday use — 196
Simplified prism — 197

INTEGRATION

It's not difficult to put together a strategy; the difficulty is remembering where you put it	202
From burning platform to big opportunity	203
Change is like riding an elephant	205

Chapter 7
Strategic hierarchy — 207

The bridge between your business strategy and brand platform	210
The elements of the pyramid	212
Mission on top	212
Values or fundamental beliefs	214
Overarching goals	223
Strategies	227
Vision	232
How do you do it?	233

Chapter 8
Strategic narrative — 237

Include everybody in the branding efforts	237
The building blocks of a good story	245
The starting point of a strategic narrative	250
Which story is the right story?	272

Nine things brand builders do well to remember	275
Thanks for your company	279
List of references	283
Keyword list	289

In the beginning

I watched the first manned mission to the moon on a black and white television set. I was six. I will never forget the seconds when the astronauts' voices faded out as they went around the moon and disappeared behind it. My friends and I held our breath until we heard the crackle once again. Man had seen the back of the moon. Now, there was nowhere we couldn't go and nothing we couldn't do.

The mission to the moon would not have been possible without a visionary American President determined to put a man on the moon and bring him safely back to earth. But it also would not have been possible without the efforts of scientists and engineers taking advantage of the newest theories and discoveries to play along with, and challenge, what the laws of nature allow.

My claim is not that brand building is exactly the same as rocket science. But nor is management, systems development, organisational change management or strategy in general. Nevertheless, within these disciplines you will find academic theory, frameworks, tools and processes that are constantly challenged and improved, to the benefit of the ambitious leaders and organisations that make use of them.

We have seen this to be the case to a particular degree over the last decade or so. The digital shift has thrown quite a few established truths overboard. For example, the new pace of innovation has made it necessary to fundamentally change the methods and tools of project management. The old tools were fine for development processes that spanned over time, perhaps even years. But now that development processes are iterative in nature and focused on continuous improvement of products and services, new tools were needed to support new ways of working.

The same shift affects branding. From a time when the brand was managed by a specific business function, it is now a concern that should be top of mind for all leaders. From exercising brand management mainly through design and communication, the brand is now built by the entire organisation. The theoretical models and processes that were fine when marketing and communications people only talked to each other, are not effective in the new situation where the brand must be understood and built through the actions of everybody.

I will admit that this is something I'm passionate about, as an entrepreneur, brand consultant, advisor and voracious reader of academic/nerdy literature. I have followed this area of academic research closely and aimed to stay up to date as new knowledge and insights have emerged. Together with colleagues and customers, we have thought, discussed, tested and adjusted. What we have found useful, we have kept, what hasn't worked has been discarded. As the collection of tried and tested methods grew, my ambition to put together a comprehensive toolbox grew as well.

Thus, this book has come to be and it is the result of 15 years of search and deploy, trial and error. I've wanted to select a portfolio of the best and most useful models, and the newest methods and knowledge we have about how to build brands today. The book is written for practical people; those who think it's worth digging a bit deeper to aim higher. It's for people who want to use the brand as leverage to take out the full potential of the organisation they work in, with or for, whether as leader, specialist, advisor or student.

For managers that don't have a marketing background, I hope the book can be an introduction to how brands can play a role in the success of the business or organisation.

For marketers, I hope the book can motivate the development of well-founded brand platforms; that it may come in handy in day to day operations and inspire in the struggle to secure an important role for the marketing function in the business.

For advisors, I hope the book can inspire the use of tools to help you do great work and motivate the search for more tools to apply to the areas that are beyond the scope of this book.

For designers and other creative forces, I think it would be wonderful if this book could contribute to more strategically executed and interpreted briefs that inspire brave branding measures that clients want and understand.

For students, my wish is primarily to inspire, but also to give you a thorough introduction to really useful brand building tools so that you might apply them to building the great brands of the future regardless of which role you aim for in your future work life.

Brand builders need tools too

My hope is that this book is picked up by everyone who thinks branding may be a strategically important resource, and want to take advantage of that resource for all it's worth.

You might say that business strategy is a kind of blueprint for building your business in the world, or «in reality». Your brand strategy is the corresponding blueprint for what you're looking to build in people's minds. Of course, the two are connected. But they are not one and the same.

In this book, you will discover a toolbox, or a collection of tools that are useful when it comes to defining your brand strategy decisions and when it comes to communicating what the decisions are. You'll find models and theories to guide you as your sort through insights; that help you structure your thoughts as well as discussions with others. You'll also find descriptions of processes that will help you make good branding decisions and communicate these decisions in a way that makes it easier to understand their consequences.

In the following I'll present you with some decisions you need to make – such as category, differentiation and identity – and some models to help you make those decisions – such as a podium, a differentiation rocket and a wheel of archetypes. It's fair to say that both the decisions themselves and the models you use to involve and inform your organisation along the way, are tools you need for the big job; namely building strong brands. I've structured it so that the chapters of this book represent each of the decisions you have to make. I introduce the models and processes to put you in a position to make those decisions within the chapters.

Which tools? And why?

There's no official standard that lays out what the end result of a brand strategy process looks like, or what it contains. As branding is not an exact science, a fixed formula may be too much to expect. It's not unfair to expect, however, a coherent system to help you get to the blueprint stage. While I have looked around, searched and read through books and articles, I have yet to discover such a coherent system in one place.

On the other hand, there's a lot of research in our field, some of it shared and popularised in ways that makes it possible to apply new insights to practical problems. Some of it has also ended up in the toolkit that is this book. What has ended up here are the insights, models and processes that have proved their worth in practical application. I've simplified some of the theory, but if you're familiar with its original source it should be easy to recognise nevertheless.

For discussions about brand across your organisation, such as what you want the brand to do for your business and how everybody's day to day contributions fit into that picture, you need practical models and tools that people can understand and apply to what they do. For that you need a common language to talk about these things, and processes that can be used across the entire organisation. This will help give people direction in their day to day decision making. Management can use this language and apply these processes to ensure that the brand is defined and developed as systematically as the other assets of your business.

The following requirements have informed my choice of which tools to include:

Insights and methods are well documented.
Where it's not been possible to tie a specific tool to a single source, an article or book, I've allowed a broader selection of sources that are recognised within our field. I will also have broad experience to confirm the tools' utility.

The tools should help you clarify and simplify in the face of complexity.
They should make the world easier to understand, the important insights stand out more clearly and show you which choices to make and what your options are. That does not mean that using the tools doesn't require effort from you. As you are probably well aware, getting to simple can be the most difficult thing in the world.

The tools must be ethical.
Brands influence our behaviours and there can be a thin line indeed between influence and manipulation. There are plenty of resources and techniques aimed at manipulation, even some that take advantage of new knowledge about the inner workings of our brain. You'll find none of those in this book.

The tools must yield results.
Not necessarily in the sense that you can expect immediate and irrefutable commercial results as such. However, the consequences of the choices you make should be much clearer and also much easier to act upon.

Just like any tool, these tools are no better than the people who make use of them, and they may require a bit of practice before you can use them for all they're worth. They work, but not of themselves.

The structure of this book

In the book's first chapter I describe the world view that underpins it. Then follows three parts. The first part treats brand positioning. The second part is devoted to brand identity. The third and final part is all about how brand strategy communication can and should be integrated with your overall strategy communication. At the very end, I offer a few pieces of advice you'd do well to consider as you go about your brand building project, whatever it might be.

There are at least three ways to read this book:
- Read it from cover to cover as an introduction to brand building, or as a refresher.
- Read individual chapters and pick up specific tools as and when you need them.
- Read the chapters as an introduction to some of the theories or thinkers you are curious about.

Whichever way works best for you; I hope you will learn something that's useful to you and that you have a good time doing it.

Chapter 1
Brands in our time

What's happened?
Brand development used to be something only marketing people did. Now it's an ongoing core strategic concern for the entire organisation. Two huge changes have caused this.

Customers are now the most important marketing channels
The first great change is that anyone can share his or her experiences with everyone and global reach can be immediate. Potential customers actively seek out information about other customers' experience before making purchasing decisions of their own. People are exposed to much more information from their peers than from people officially communicating on behalf of the brand. In addition, what other people are saying is more

"a big lump of metal"

◉○○○○ Aug 23, 2007

 **deenkies (17 reviews)**
ireland

Now, i'm not being picky here. I like to give fair, often kind reviews, BUT...what an eyesore!!! Looked uglier than in the pictures and wouldnt impress my easily-impressed great granny! Boring and expensive with alot of wheeler-deelers around the base

Needless to say i remain unimpressed with the eiffel tower

Helpful?   2   Thank deenkies

credible and more likely to influence our decisions (Court et. al. 2009). That's why brands must work very hard to motivate people to become their advocates and share positive brand experiences. Consequently, everyone's brand experiences have the potential to play a part in building the brand; their experiences with the brand will also colour their interpretation of the brands' own communication. This applies across the brand experience, starting from the very first consideration of it, and continuing with purchase, delivery, use, return, customer support, recycling and onto possibly another purchase. This means that everyone who works in the organisation across all of these functions, must understand the brand they represent, so that they are able to deliver a consistent brand experience.

Because existing customers now have this critical role in attracting new customers, leading brands are shifting their marketing efforts from traditional pre-purchase activities, which are aimed at influencing the purchasing decision, to placing greater emphasis on the actual post-purchase customer experience.

Nike was one of the first global brands to take this seriously. The cost of developing, producing and marketing the first wearable activity monitor came out of, and almost gobbled up, a full year's marketing budget. However, the Nike FuelBand led people to register on Nike + with all the advantages that gave them and Nike. Nike could harvest data about how people actually work out, communicate directly with users and cheer people on if, for example, they had an unusually active week.

This is not at all easy. For customers to find the motivation to say nice things about your brand, you have to really wow them. It may seem unfair that you can do everything right and fulfil all their expectations and get so little appreciation in return, but look what you find on TripAdvisor. The super happy, and equally unhappy, customers dominate. Exceptional experiences move people to advocate. To trigger a reaction from customers, you'll have to surprise them a bit, preferably in a positive way.

Consider Netflix. New customers sign up for the service after discussions about the films and shows they run. Not the terms of its streaming subscription service, because who talks about that sort of thing? Instead, it starts with someone asking whether you have seen such and such a show? All of a sudden you feel left out of the conversation and, gripped by fear of missing out, you sign up. To further increase the gap between people in the know and others, Netflix started producing its own series, not just distributing content from others. If the shows are addictive enough, Netflix can rest assured that the viewers will do the marketing for them.

The speed of innovation is higher, and competition more complex

The other great shift is one of tempo, innovation and industry fluidity. Traditionally, brand development and marketing have been weapons wielded in the battle for market share in a relatively stable competitive arena of products and services, customer segments and competitors. Coke and Pepsi have competed for thirsty consumers for generations, each bouncing their distribution power and market communication efforts off the other in a fairly predictable way. And so did newspapers, banks, car manufacturers and so on, using the relatively unchanging means of competition at their disposal.

Today, the picture is a lot fuzzier. Services previously delivered by one kind of brand, may suddenly come from a different kind of source altogether, such as credit cards from your coffee vendor, or cars from your search engine provider. New product categories are launched, lost and rediscovered. Long after vinyl records were relegated to a bygone era, the category has been revitalised as a music lover status symbol and hipster artefact.

We used to talk about brand promises, or that a brand represented a set of associations. Unfortunately, associations can become irrelevant very quickly in a rapidly changing market. Once upon a time and not that long ago, we all had very clear association to the Kodak brand. It was yellow and red, and clearly associated with square boxes with film containers, and envelopes with photos and negatives. Kodak owned moments worth remembering, known, in fact, as "Kodak Moments". And yet, Kodak went bust. Images are no longer just for unforgettable moments collected in photo albums or framed and hung on the wall. Snapshots are now an integral part of the way we communicate, a fleeting everyday matter. Associations are no longer sufficient. Today, we should aim at building brands that people want to associate with, and form an attachment to; this leaves the brand less exposed in times of change. As long as a brand you feel you have a relation to is able to deliver in accordance with your evolving expectations, the relationship may endure.

The closer the relationship between brand and customer, the better. Associations and promises may change in brand relationships, just as in human relationships. The boy next door became a friend, a boyfriend, a fellow student, a spouse, a father and so on. Associations change, the relationship remains and continues to develop. Similarly, a brand where the entire organisation has a good understanding of the kind of relationship its customers want to have with the brand can look for ways to strengthen that relationship in a very consistent and focused manner when exploring new products or services as well.

Netflix had built a strong brand as a DVD sales and rental company and was able to maintain its relationship with its customers, as well as reach new ones, as it transitioned to the new content distribution model – streaming. The further expansion of its brand from content distribution to Netflix original content production was another way of strengthening that brand relationship, especially as the viewers deemed the quality of its films and television series more than acceptable and yet another reason to stay with the brand.

As brands find new ways of taking advantage of the relationship people are willing to have with them, much more than pursuing a single promise or set of associations, we see online commerce giant Alibaba become the world's largest bank, and the coffeehouse chain Starbucks with more customer money on its cards than many banks have in deposits.

A new role – and a new definition – for brands

Recognition of this new consumer power, has led us to a new understanding about what brands are today. The definition of "brand" has been updated before in line with changes in what a brand actually does for products, services and organisations. It's time to do so again. As mentioned, the prevalent definition of brand is still the one formulated by the American brand guru Keller in 1998: "A brand is a set of associations in the mind of the consumer". However, Jean-Noël Kapferer, leading brand thinker in Europe, has suggested the following as an updated definition: A brand is a name with the power to influence (Kapferer 2012, p. 11). In his book *The New Strategic Brand Management*, he states that it is a brand's ability to influence individuals as well as entire markets over time that makes brands both relevant and strong.

Tesla, Nike and eBay are strong brands also by yesterday's definition, but it's these brands' ability to change our behaviour and the role we allow them to play in our lives that are their real strengths.

When I claim that it is the relationship the brand is able to establish with its customers and users that is the new foundation for strong brands, it is based on my understanding of Kapferer's brand definition and its emphasis on influence. People are not influenced to a significant degree by people they don't know or like, and not at all by people they dislike (Cialdini 2006). Thus, a brand's ability to build and develop a familiar relationship with people has become a prerequisite to its success.

If eBay helps me get rid of something I no longer need, or make some extra cash on the side, that makes me like eBay more. And if I start to really like eBay, I may talk about it to people I know. My relationship with eBay says something about me that I like, and because I like what eBay does for me, I will want people I know to have the same opportunity.

In November 2015, Harvard Business Review published the first in a series of articles with findings from an 8-year-long study of 4000 brands, across more than 30 industries, analysing a billion data points. The first finding comes as no great surprise. Customers that have an emotional relationship with a brand – in a positive way – are on average 52 per cent more valuable than customers who are simply very happy with it. The main reason they are so much more valuable is that the people who are emotional about a brand are that much more likely to advocate on behalf of it. Satisfied customers usually don't bother.

A brand is a name with the power to influence

Jean-Noël Kapferer

The New Strategic Brand Management, 2012

Consequently, a brand's power to influence depends on its ability to build and maintain relationships with customers, users, talent markets or other interested parties.

New times call for new tools

The ability to build brands has been a business critical skill for a long time. It is well documented through numerous studies and rankings that strong brands lead to loyalty, make it possible to demand a premium price and attract the best talent. In other words, a strong brand is one of several means towards achieving a goal, whether that goal is a profitable business or some other mission. Some brand investments are more successful than others. In my opinion, taking advantage of new insights and new tools will increase the probability that your brand investments yield a proper return.

The way organisations work to develop brands has changed, but despite this, the theoretical framework used across industries, functions and different levels of management as well as the models used to guide their marketing efforts, have changed very little. What I have come across most often over the past 15 years looks more or less like this:
- The marketing mix (McCarthy 1960) is used a lot, especially for discussions at the product/service level.
- The sales funnel, or AIDA-model (Lewis 1903) is probably the closest thing we have to a universally accepted cross industry model. Most major brands measure awareness, interest and desire.
- The USP (Unique selling point) (Levitt 1986, but apparently hails from the 1940s) is also a term commonly thrown around and most brands, at least the ones I have seen background materials on, will include some variant of this concept.

- The identity prism model (Kapferer 2012) does come up from time to time, but most brand identities are described with reference to personality traits and through the use of analogies.
- Models aimed at helping brand builders capture the entire brand, such as Kotler & Keller's *Brand equity model* (Kotler and Keller et. al., 2015), Aaker & Joachimstaler's *Brand Identity Planning Model* (Aaker and Joachimstaler 2000) and Unilever's *Brand Key*. However, it is rare to see either of these applied to anything other than pure consumer goods brands.

SWOTs, value mapping and prototypes

Other business disciplines have much richer and more comprehensive theoretical frameworks with which their practitioners will be familiar; be these well-established models and methods like value chains, SWOT-analyses and BCG-matrixes, or newer varieties like Business Model Generation (Osterwalder and Pigneur 2010), strategy map (Kaplan and Norton 2004) or Design Thinking (Brown 2009). Staying up to date on current thinking in your field is the professional thing to do and may be a competitive advantage in the jostle for key roles in a business, attractive positions in the job market or consulting assignments.

This is not to the same extent the case for marketing functions. Could it be because the brand building profession is associated more with its creative expressions or advertising campaigns, than its underlying strategic rationale?

Either way, the time when a marketing department could outsource the management of its brand(s) to a selection of "creatives" outside the organisation is certainly long gone.

In our new reality, brands must be tied closely to the overall business strategy, all of management must be seen to stand behind it and contribute towards furthering the brand building effort. And, because brands are built first and foremost in day-to-day operations, the entire organisation needs to be on board and motivated to play a part in making the brand consistent and strong. The marketing function will still be the hub of the branding efforts, but today the brand is built, maintained and developed by everybody, all the time. It goes without saying that we need a common language, a jointly understood method and a shared set of tools to bring this about, much more so today than just a decade or so ago.

Luckily, this all exists, and we'll get to it shortly. However, before going into the tools and methods described in this book specifically, I'd like to present two fundamental insights. The first is to do with the customer journey; the second insight is to do with a more dynamic strategy paradigm.

The customer decision journey is the new sales funnel

McKinsey published its first article about the customer decision journey in 2009. In this article, they claimed rather forcefully, that the old way of thinking about marketing not only doesn't help, but actually stands in the way of establishing lasting customer relationships.

The old model portrays the customer decision process much like a funnel. The thinking goes like this: when potential customers contemplate a purchase, they start with a set of known alternatives that they can then evaluate. Through a process of evaluation,

The old and a new model describing customers' decision making prosess

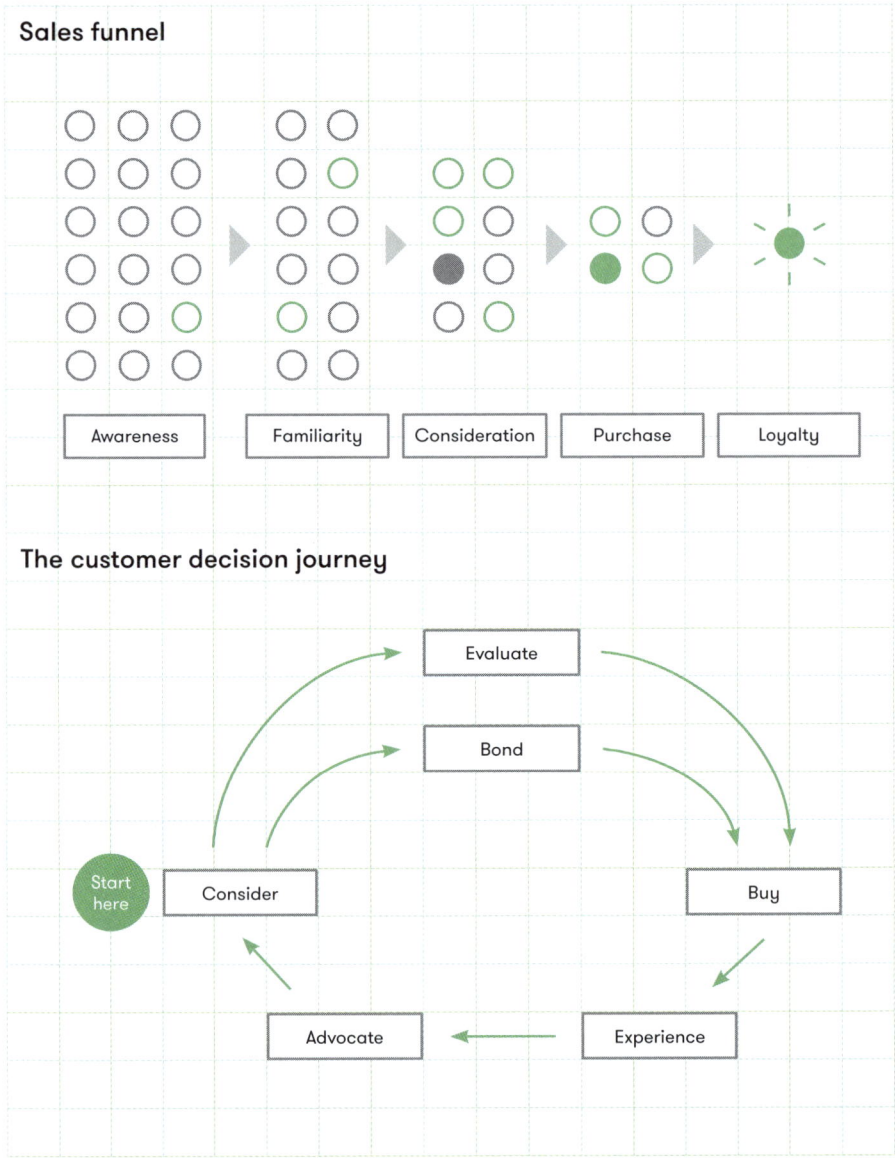

Source: McKinsey 2009

one-by-one the alternatives will be eliminated until, based on their set of emotional and functional criteria, only one alternative remains and a purchasing decision will have been made.

This understanding of the purchasing decision journey is the rationale behind the traditional split between emotional, brand building campaigns that are seen as separate from more functional, sales-triggering campaigns. Where the first type of campaign aims at making sure your brand is on the list of alternatives to be considered, the second kind of campaign is meant to kick-start a purchasing process.

However, this is no longer the best approach to understanding the purchasing process. We know that potential customers don't start out with an exhaustive list of brands to consider. Alternatives are added and taken off the list throughout the process all the way up to the final decision. Being on the list from the get-go may have its advantages, but we know that people actively seek new alternatives until the end. A customer's previous experience with a brand, as well as that of others, has more impact on willingness to buy than traditional marketing messages. As early as 2009, when McKinsey published their findings from the customer decision journey study, they could document that about two-thirds of the information people received before making a purchasing decision came from sources other than the brand itself.

In later updates from their study, McKinsey showed us that it is our friends who influence us the most. We are also more likely to be influenced by others during a first-time purchase, before we have experienced a brand first-hand and made up our own mind about it. Perhaps this does not strike you as radically new information. After all, word-of-mouth has always been important. What's new is the volume, the easy access and systematic presentation of

Kapferer's social positioning

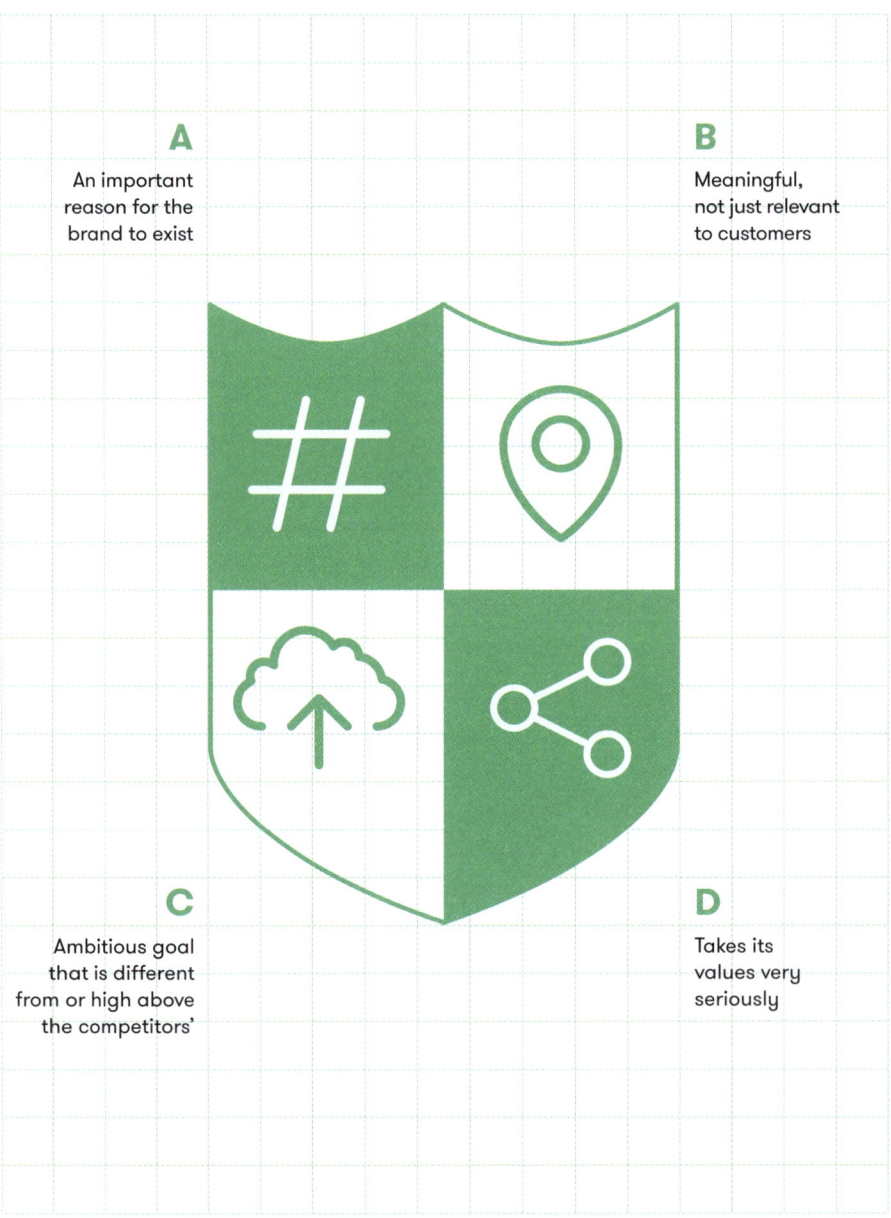

A An important reason for the brand to exist

B Meaningful, not just relevant to customers

C Ambitious goal that is different from or high above the competitors'

D Takes its values very seriously

Kapferer (2012), p. 154–164

word-of-mouth testimonies. Also new is our increasingly pragmatic attitude towards switching brands. The travel and hospitality industries are feeling this very keenly, with the importance of user evaluation platforms like TripAdvisor, Yelp and others increasing day-by-day.

In light of this development, the only sensible thing to do is to allocate marketing spending across the entire decision journey. This entails a shift in focus, from always vying for attention, to viewing your marketing efforts as that which helps your brand be attractive throughout the customer experience, strengthening the relationship between user and the brand along the way.

The McKinsey model was further refined in 2015, now showing how the best brand builders work systematically to establish a relationship with potential customers even before their first purchase. That sense of having a relationship with a brand, whether people are customers yet or not, has some obvious advantages in a purchasing or selection process. While most of us have yet to experience an Uber ride, or stay/host with Airbnb, it's clear that any perceived bond with either brand could work in their favour if and when the day comes for us to try these kinds of services.

From a static to a dynamic strategy paradigm

It's been a while since Michael Porter, the world's most influential business strategy thinker, stated that the time is over when a static approach to strategy was sufficient. The markets themselves are simply too dynamic for that to fly. His argument was to replace the static approach with one that is more dynamic and company specific (Porter 1996).

Under this dynamic strategy paradigm, the brand must also develop and revitalise continuously. This shift in approach has consequences in terms of what we need our tools to do for us and we need to learn how to use them in new ways. Strategy in general is outside of the scope of this book – it's such a huge subject on its own. In this book we will stick to brand strategy to the extent that it is possible to treat this subject in isolation.

Kapferer described the shift strategy paradigm for brands as a shift from *why* a brand exists to what a brand *wants to achieve* (2012, p. 154–164). We are talking about a social positioning for brands. A social positioning is an excellent starting point for brands that want to build a relationship with people in order to influence them more effectively.

This means that people working to build brands must shift their mind-set so they can more effectively communicate not so much what the brand *is* but what it *wants*.

A much-used acid test for brand positioning has the following requirements:
- It should be relevant to customers
- Believable in the category
- Differentiated from competitors
- Possible for the brand to carry off

While still valid, this acid test is no longer sufficient. It's necessary to think more holistically, and generally create more enthusiasm, if the objective is the power to influence and strong customer relationships. This is an updated checklist for well-executed brand positioning:
- An important reason to exist – a cause or battle the brand is fighting on behalf of us all. The brand's "Why are we"?
- An ambitious goal or objective that is different from, or high above, the goals of its competitors.

- Aim to be meaningful, not just relevant to customers.
- Will not compromise on its values and is dead serious about what the brand stands for.

Now, finally, the toolbox

The tools described in this book take the new brand definition, as well as our new insight about how people establish emotional relationships with brands, as a starting point.

We begin with what Kapferer calls a brand platform (2012, p. 156). A brand platform consists of two things: the brand's identity and the positioning that will give the brand the best possible chance of winning in its market.

The positioning tools define *what* the brand is and *in what way*.
- What is the brand's category or which category does it aim to establish in people's minds.
- Which role does the brand play in its category? (Is it a category leader, a challenger to the leader, or about to redefine a category or its rules?)
- In what way is the brand different from its competitors?

The identity tools define *who* the brand is by exploring:
- What motivates people to relate to the brand?
- What is the brand personality, what is shared by the brand and its users, and how does the relationship to the brand affect the users' perceptions of their own identity?

To make sure the brand strategy discussion is fully integrated in the overall business strategy discussion, thereby becoming a motivating force within the organisation, we have added two integration tools. These tools are particularly useful for management teams that want to be loud and clear in their communication when explaining to everybody how the brand building effort is everybody's business. The tools are for those who realise that brand building is too important to be left to only a single function of the organisation. These integration tools can be described as follows:

- A strategic hierarchy organised in a pyramid of familiar business strategy components such as mission, vision, goals, strategies and values, only this time viewed from a brand perspective. When the elements are properly defined, the pyramid will function as the bridge uniting your brand platform and your business strategy. It's a one-page representation of your business' direction and ambitions.
- A strategic narrative outlining your brand's next big story. In a world where brands are built by all the people, it helps when all the people have a sense of what story they are part of as well as their individual part in it. Understanding the greater narrative makes it easier to have an intuitive grasp of how each person's day-to-day job fits in and contributes towards moving the story forward.

The brand positioning and strategy pyramid tools are structural and in the management's domain. Management is responsible for setting the direction as well as the goals for the organisation. Changes may be large or small, rapid or gradual. Either way, management sets both pace and direction for the organisation whether all the employees like it or not.

The brand identity and the strategic narrative are cultural tools and thereby in everybody's domain. Culture changes slowly. It's the culture that determines which values and actions are merely acceptable and which are applauded. Within the culture live the heroes and the stories that for all purposes determine how customers experience the brand relationship.

It's the sum of the actions defined by the strategy and realised within the culture, that builds the brand by shaping the stories, attitudes and relationships to the brand's most important marketing channel – its customers.

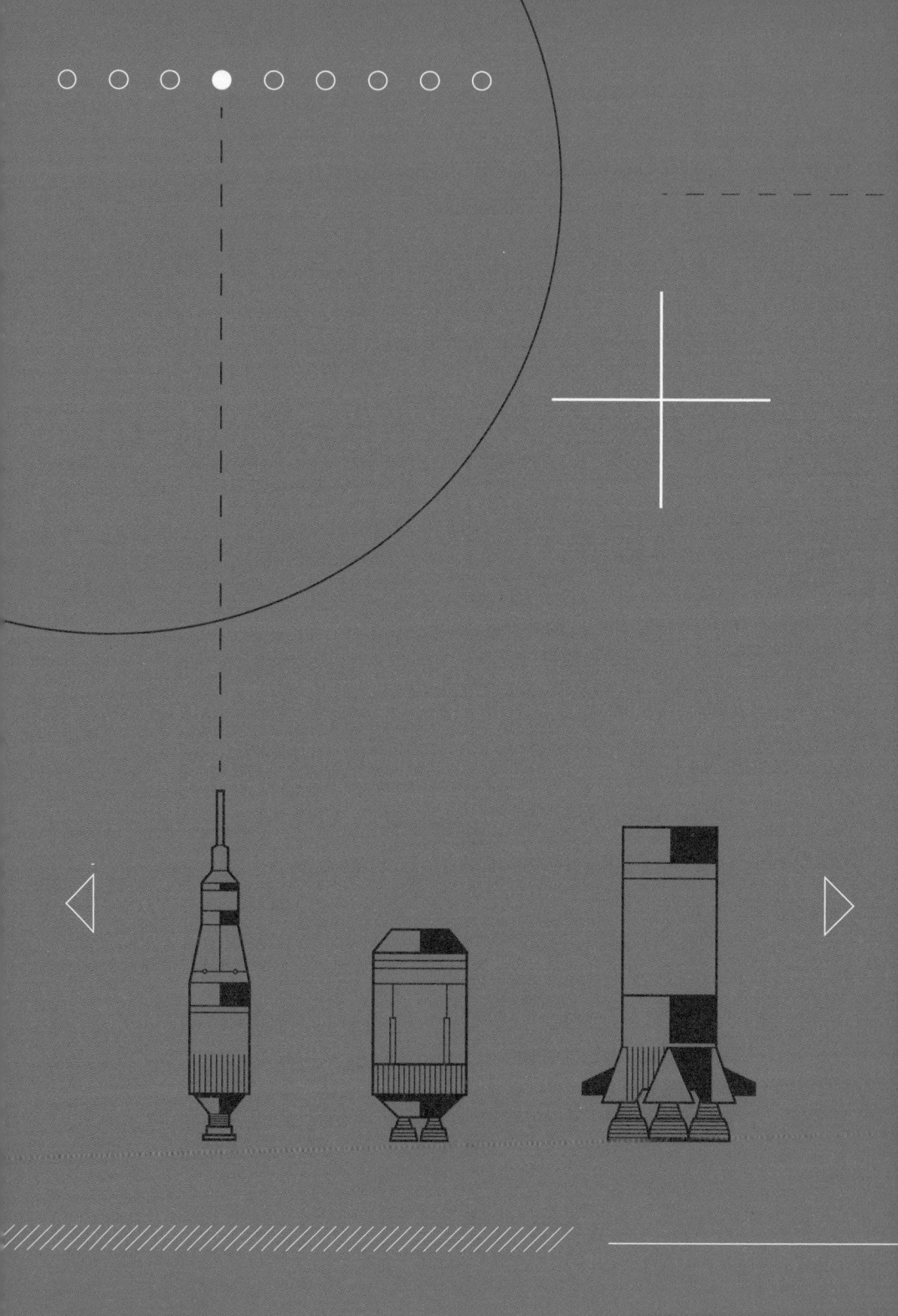

Positioning

Category

 Role

Differentiation

Brands exist in our minds

Canon   patagonia   BRITISH AIRWAYS

Nikon   THE NORTH FACE   AIRFRANCE /

FUJIFILM   HH HELLY HANSEN RYANAIR

        NETFLIX   CHANEL

        HBO   M·A·C

        BBC   Yves Saint Laurent

A brand among other things
No brand is an island. Brands exist in parallel with other brands. You will find brands wherever there is competition for market share, the attention of politicians, visibility, credibility or gravitas. You will find brands wherever there is competition for people's time, attention and recognition.

The theories and methods described in this book are not about business strategy as such. However, we will consider brands from a competition perspective, so looking closely at what is going on in the competitive arena is crucial.

A brand strategy that is not rooted in a solid business strategy, or a clear purpose, is almost unthinkable. I have yet to see a strong brand that does not have a business strategy as its secure and solid foundation. So, I argue that it is useful for builders of brands to look to strategy development, and its models and methods with a friendly eye. Porter (1996) makes use of the terms *rivals* and *substitutes* when discussing competition. It can be useful both to look at rival brands that threaten your role in your category (for example your market leadership) as well as substitute brands that call into question the relevance of the category itself. The competitive arena for a brand is defined by the pool of relevant alternative brands, as seen by potential customers.

Positioning a brand is thus all about establishing what category, role and differentiation will give it the best possible chance of playing a part in people's lives.

Chapter 2
Category – the door to people's minds

It happens that people give me a strange look when I insist on starting any brand strategy process by a discussion of the brand's category. Can this really be necessary? Indeed, it is. In today's slippery markets, the question of category is perhaps the most important one of all. Unless we fully understand a brand's category, any efforts to build the brand are as good as wasted.

Let's start at the beginning – a couple of million years ago. Imagine that you are an ape-like Homo Habilis on the great African savannah. Your brain is about half the size of your current brain. You're carrying a spear and walking along with your fellow hunters. You're moving quietly through the tall grass. Your peripheral vision picks up movement. In an instant your small brain must make a life or death decision: is it a boar's tail (= dinner) or a lion's tail (= we are dinner)? Or is it just the grass, a stick, or some other harmless object? Your call will determine whether your tribe gets to eat, is eaten or goes hungry until the next opportunity for food presents itself.

Categorisation must be quick as lightning, but does not have to go into great detail. The ability to categorise, and separate lion, boar and grass, for example, is one of the earliest jobs our brains learned to perform, hundreds of thousands of years before we developed our "modern" brain.

This is why the ability to categorise is found in the oldest part of our brain. More sophisticated functions, such as characterisation, comparison, evaluation, and preference came later and are located in newer parts of our brain.

Brands according to the brain

Recent discoveries in the primacy of category can be useful to brand builders. Scientists Antzoulatos and Miller (2011) scanned the brains of monkeys learning to sort patterns into categories, and their research showed that the monkeys formed category-specific connections in the brain when they acquired new categories. These learned category connections influence how we perceive the world around us.

We used to think that the brain perceives something by first becoming aware of it, then evaluating it and assigning it to a category. On the contrary, say scientists today. Stuff must go via the categorising part of the brain before we can evaluate it. We acquire new categories through the experience of a sufficient number of instances of something that the brain invests in a category-specific connection. This takes time and is pretty hard work for the brain. However, once a category is established, sorting new instances is easy. Even a one-year-old will efficiently, and usually fairly precisely, sort cats from dogs. Thus, not belonging to a category is a great disadvantage for a brand, given that relating to a thing without a category is so much harder work for the brain. Worst case, people will select not to relate at all, as if "blind" to your brand.

Take the following situation: Around the coffee machine people are discussing the latest TV-series. You feel left out because the channels on your TV aren't running a particular show yet. One could imagine that you start considering subscribing to Netflix or HBO and that your next move is to evaluate their relative merits in terms of cost and quality and make your selection. Next you observe that this is something different to traditional TV-channels and categorise this new thing as streaming services. In fact, that's not quite how it works. Before people can start evaluating the relative merits of different streaming services, the category must already be on their radar.

Our little situation above changes as follows: People are discussing TV-series. You understand that the time has come for you to relate to streaming services for films and TV-shows, much like you did a while ago when you had to make the choice whether to continue to buy music CDs, buy music from iTunes or enter the uncertain world of music streaming. Once you decide TV show streaming is a thing you should relate to, you can evaluate the different services and decide which one to choose. You don't want to be clueless by the coffee machine after all.

Maybe this doesn't seem like a big difference, but it is. Scientists say that unless we go via category, our brains simply don't want to see things. Unless your brand belongs to a clear category, it doesn't exist in people's minds. So before you go any further in your brand building efforts, make sure you have a rock solid answer to the question: What is it?

The King of Category

Steve Jobs, former CEO and co-founder of Apple, understood the importance of category better than most. If your ambition is to put a dent in the universe, simply making better products than your competitors will not do. One has to create products that are something new entirely. And when you do that, you have to do two things at once – introduce a new category and introduce its reference product at the same time.

Steve Jobs did it with his "one more thing", the operative word being thing. It was a signal that here comes something new. In a matter of minutes, Steve Jobs had to establish a new category and explain to us why we should be interested in it. His next job was to sell the product, and sell it to the extent that we were willing to line up around the block to get our hands on it.

A few examples of how he did just that below:
- **iPod:** "Music player. […] With iPod, Apple has invented a whole new category of digital music player that lets you put your entire music collection in your pocket and listen to it wherever you go." (Apple 2001)
- **iPhone:** "The ultimate digital device. […] It is a revolutionary mobile phone, a widescreen iPod with touch controls and a breakthrough Internet communications device." (Apple 2007) This may be the only category we did not let him name. The ultimate digital device was too pompous to be a category designation and Apple had to accept the well-established smartphone term.
- **iPad:** "A tablet. […] Our most advanced technology in a magical and revolutionary device at an unbelievable price." (Apple 2010)

Category properties and brand properties

In addition to making sure your brand exists in people's minds, there is another benefit to belonging to a clear category; namely that people are already familiar with general category traits. People will know things about your brand that you don't have to tell them. The category itself forms people's expectations and automatically assigns properties to your brand. This means that as a brand builder, you can focus all your energy on communicating how your brand stands out in the category and not waste your breath on what's already given. You'd do well to remember this. An overwhelming number of brands don't and waste bandwidth and resources on stating the obvious.

Take the legal profession as a case in point. You don't have to look far to find lofty expressions about understanding clients' needs, about ethical standards and knowledge of the law. Really? This belongs to the category and should go without saying. Why not say something about how your law firm brand is different from other law firm brands? Or how your firm acts in a way that is different to how other law firms act?

Here's how BA-HR has chosen, as an expression of the brand's positioning, to say something about its particular strength as a business law firm:

Small teams for big matters

What BA-HR is doing here is tell people that it is the kind of firm that puts highly effective teams to work on the really important cases. They do more than that, of course, but this is what they want people to remember and its brand to represent.

Category kings take it upon themselves to design a great product, a great company and a great category at the same time.

Al Ramadan, Dave Peterson, Christopher Lochhead and Kevin Maney

Play Bigger, 2016

Naming a category

We now know that category is necessary to deserve a place in people's minds. We also know that we attribute general traits to categories, such as lion = lethal and boar = survival. Both insights are useful to brand builders, in particular if you take on the job of naming a category.

Chatbot, crowdsourcing, music streaming, and social media are all examples illustrating how by naming a category you also get to define some of its associated properties.

Giving a category its name is the greatest privilege of whoever establishes the new category in people's minds. If anybody still remembers WAP (mobile Internet in its infancy), take that as a prime example of how not to go about naming a category. Few people knew or cared about the technology itself, making the job of filling the acronym for Wireless Application Protocol with any meaningful content an uphill struggle indeed. People just wanted to browse the Internet on their phones.

In contrast, Google has named the category for cars-that-drive-without-an-actual-driver-behind-the-wheel with the term self-driving cars, rather than say robotic cars. Self-driving sounds wonderful. You can relax and safely leave navigation to a computer that knows the best roads to everywhere, has sensors that see everything and never gets tired. A robotic car on the other hand sounds like something that can be hacked, have software glitches and, worst case, drive off with our kids. The categories robotic mower and robotic vacuum cleaner are fine, but robotic cars – no thank you.

When it comes to brands, it works pretty much like this: Whichever brand is first to establish a category in people's minds will also determine which properties will be attributed to the category. The brand that establishes the category also establishes and typically takes ownership of the most important selection criteria. This leaves other brands to compete on the less important criteria. Whole Foods owns natural and organic food. Ryanair owns cheap flights. Competitors must match, exceed or find other ways to deliver on people's expectations to the category.

Category and the competitive arena

According to the immutable laws of marketing (Ries and Ries, 2002) whoever is first to establish a category in people's minds will win the category. It's not enough to be first in market, but first to represent the category in the minds of consumers.

Notice how great businesses and brands often choose a fast follower strategy, leaving the hard work of being first mover to smaller players and/or entrepreneurs. As soon as a new category is starting to show promise and has attracted a critical mass of users, the big players have a tendency to devour the small, or enter the competitive arena with a similar product. Because they are already big, they will have existing customer relationships to lean on. Because they also typically have bigger marketing and distribution muscles, they are able to make the category more visible, seem more secure and relevant to the masses. Smaller players that have resisted acquisition must seek refuge in a category niche to survive. This is typically how it goes, unless the giants are asleep. If you snooze you lose, and the next generation of giants are only too happy to take over when they can. With this in mind, it's interesting to note that the average age of the world's 100 most valuable companies dropped by 16 years – from 84 to 68 – between 2006 and 2012 (Millward Brown, 2012).

Three strategies

When defining a category for your brand, these strategies are your best options:

1. Accept the market leader's category definition

If your brand is the market leader – great. In that case, your job is to make sure you maintain the power to define the category. You do that by referring to the category by name as often as you can, establishing and making use of a category vocabulary, and telling category-cultivating stories. If your brand is a challenger in the market, you will usually have to abide by the category rules set by the market leader. Take Pepsi in the cola category, a challenger to market-leading brand Coca-Cola, and without a clear sub category of cola to dominate. Hence Pepsi challenges Coke by being a distinctly different brand alternative (for the new generation) in the category, all the while fulfilling the selection requirements in the market based on expectations set by Coke.

2. Split the category by defining a clear sub category

This tends to happen in all categories as they grow in size and number of brands. As a market grows, viable opportunities for specialisation will emerge. It can go something like this: First you'll have one chain of gyms and a challenger brand to it. As the category becomes more crowded, specialist brands start to appear, such as unmanned gyms (low-price) or gyms that are more like spas (= luxury) shaving off the top and the bottom of the category.

3. Establish a new category

In our tumultuous time, with constant technological innovation and correspondingly new business models, we find need of – and opportunities in – establishing new categories. As a rule, something like this happens: a product or service emerges that is so different from what we are used to that we struggle to place it in a familiar industry or product category. Airbnb is not quite a sub category of hotel accommodation. Private hotel sounds shady, and short term rental not very appealing. The Airbnb brand is a spin on the familiar concept of a Bed and Breakfast, where people rent out a room, or several rooms, in their home. The first name for the brand was AirBed & Breakfast – a brilliant name stumbled upon by two students who rented out an airbed in their flat for much needed cash. And voila, an old category was reinvented in a new format, a success formula well-known by crafty entrepreneurs. Red Bull was launched as a beverage that gives you wings, not as a beverage that gives you energy – as that category attribute belongs to sports beverages such as Gatorade. Today, sports drinks and – strangely perhaps – energy drinks are still two separate categories.

Deciding what a category is all about

Working with category definition, it's important to keep it real. It can be tempting, in the spirit of innovation, to define a category so new that people just don't get it. If you feel yourself getting carried away, take a moment to consider whether clearly differentiating your brand from its competitors in an existing category that people know, and that comes with a ready set of expectations and associations, might be a better option.

Let's take a look at the electric car category. In the early days electric cars were small, funny looking and neither particularly safe or comfortable to drive. Small, unattractive and unsafe became attributes associated with the electric car category. So when Tesla launched its first car, the Roadster, it was launched as a sports car. The sports car category has a very different set of associations when it comes to driving qualities, looks, price point and sex appeal

❝ **In short, category is at the very root of brand building. It should be absolutely forbidden to proceed to differentiation and identity before your brand has got its category right.**

that the Roadster, as a sports car, had to deliver. The fact that the Roadster has an electric motor became a differentiator within the sports car category, rather than a category-defining attribute. Alternatively, Tesla could have launched the Roadster as a game changer within the electric car category, where its coolness in combination with benefits to our climate could have provided many of us with a good excuse for choosing a sports car.

Nevertheless, Tesla-models are still talked about as electric cars, but the car categories are most likely going the way of the telephone category. First there was only the telephone, then we had telephone and mobile phone, then we had fixed line phone and mobile phone, and now we are back to just phone, which of course is mobile.

A certain level of sobriety is advisable if your goal is to change people's category perceptions. Even if your product or service is indeed innovative enough to break the boundaries of all know categories, establishing the new one in people's minds will usually require tremendous resources in terms of time and money. Ryanair, however, is a well-known example showing that the effort can be worth it. By establishing the low price carrier category in Europe, the brand has reigned in a category of its own for years. Traditional

It's not the tools that you have faith in – tools are just tools. They work, or they don't work. It's people you have faith in or not.

Steve Jobs

Roling Stone Magazine, 1994

carriers have scrambled to establish low cost subsidiaries, enduring round after painful round of cost cutting and conflict, to be able to compete. All the while, Ryanair has kept the power to define what constitutes a low-cost carrier in Europe, much like Southwest Airlines who established and continues to dominate the category in the US has done.

As before, when naming a new (sub) category, choose the name wisely. Sometimes it's easy because the brand is aimed at a specific target group (children's clothing), selection criterion (low cost airfares), level of quality (gourmet food), size (mini-SUV) or similar. Other times the category shift is more fundamental, which may allow use of the anchor and twist strategy (Heath and Heath 2008). When you anchor and twist, you anchor your brand to something that is known of a category and twist it over to explain how it applies in your "new" category. Such as, "we're like Airbnb, only for cars" or "We are like Spotify for books".

In short, category is at the very root of brand building. It should be absolutely forbidden to proceed to differentiation and identity before your brand has got its category right. The category discussion must be based on which positions you have reason to believe will be attractive in the future, given changes happening in and around your brand's competitive arena.

Chapter 3
Role

Put simply, brands are substitutes for, or replace the personal relationship between manufacturers and consumers of the past – baker, cobbler and farmer alike. Thus it applies to brands as much as to people that our expectations of them vary depending on the situation, the nature of our relationship and the role they play. We all have an overall personality, but we will adapt and adjust our behaviour depending on the nature of the relationship we have with whoever we are with, and the situation we are in. There's a difference between hanging out with a pal, a supplier or a parent, and we behave differently at a party, at work or a funeral. Some of these roles are more stable and long lasting.

Two clear roles – and one other option

When it comes to brands, two roles in particular come with clear norms, and brands violate our expectations at their peril.

Positioning

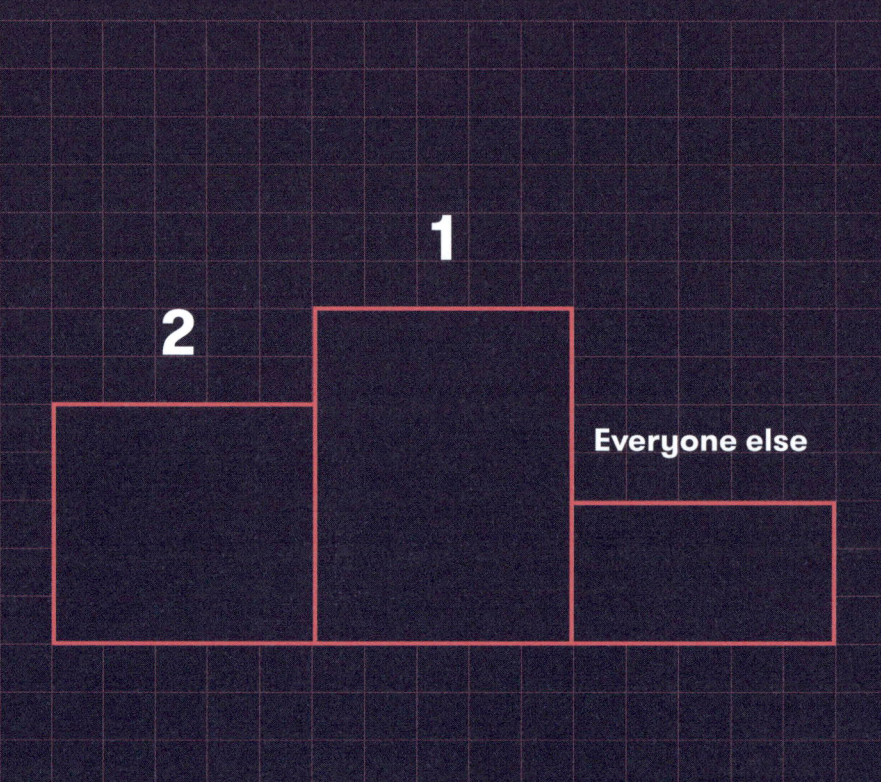

The Market leader

The market leader has the greatest market share and is the most profitable brand in the category. Market leaders often take "ownership" of the most important selection criterion, and has the resources and responsibility to innovate on behalf of the entire category.

The Challenger

The challenger is, or aims to be, the second most dominant brand. A challenger is positioned as a clear alternative to the market leader by being different in a specific way and/or on specific selection criteria.

Everyone else

Brands that are neither the leader or the recognised challenger to the leader, have a hard time achieving visibility in a category.

These are the market leader and the challenger roles. Often, I will demonstrate the relative strengths of a market leader and its challenger in a category by placing them on a podium, with the market leader on the top, the challenger in second place and all other brands on the bronze level. In addition to these roles, we see a third emerging, which we refer to as the pioneer.

Being aware of a brand's role in a category is important because the role comes with some rules. Unless the role is well defined when you position your brand, you may fall into the trap where your brand's identity simply mirrors the category's identity. What we really want is a brand that's clearly differentiated from other brands in the category. Understanding your brand's role in the category is also essential when it comes to crafting an exciting and credible narrative for your brand; a brand story people can relate to.

The market leader and challenger roles are well known to us from the epic brand wars of Coke and Pepsi, Hertz and Avis, and McDonalds and Burger King. We also see this dynamic play out in the current competitive arena by brands such as Apple vs. Samsung, Nike vs. Adidas and Nintendo vs. PlayStation.

Today, however, the categories have become more dynamic, so who competes with whom changes rapidly and may vary from category to category for brands that compete in more than one. For example, we consider Google a challenger to Microsoft on Office-like products such as Docs, Sheets and Slides. At the same time, Google is clearly the global market leader when it comes to search, and that dominance sets some boundaries for how it is acceptable for Google to behave that are separate from the boundaries set by laws and regulation.

Why two roles?

The market leader and challenger roles are the two visible roles in a category. Why only two? Probably because there's a limited number of selection criteria that really matter to people. The brands that are able to seize ownership of the top criteria typically win. The market leader and challenger roles are often established as the category is formed, the market leader specializing in catering to the customers' most important criterion, and the challenger taking ownership of the second one. Being viewed as the best brand for the most important criterion gives the market leader great advantages. The brand is selected most frequently, which means it's in a position to build relationships with more customers and cement preferences in the market. This, in turn, gives the market leader distribution power and economy of scale advantages, as well as resources to hire the best people and invest in innovation. As a result, the market leader can keep improving its offering and operations, amassing ever greater resources relative to its competitors.

We often look to arch rivals Coca-Cola and Pepsi as prime representatives of the market leader vs. challenger dynamic. Coca-Cola presents itself as the original (the real thing) in accordance with market leader conventions. It further assumes a market leader role by talking about the joys of drinking a fizzy drink, how we must all make sure to have enough cola on stock, that cola goes well with food and belongs to the sphere of family and good times. Pepsi, the challenger, rarely talks about when it is appropriate to drink cola. Pepsi says that Pepsi tastes better than Coke (as proven in many a blind testing Pepsi challenge) and that Pepsi represents a more youthful culture than stilted old Coca-Cola.

Even in markets where Pepsi actually has the largest market share, the brand assumes the challenger position of being an alternative to Coca-Cola. And less we forget, other colas do exist – for example Carma Cola (New Zealand/UK), Afri-Cola (Germany), Jolt Cola (just re-launched in the US) and Mecca Cola (France) and numerous local brands, but unless you're in a very specific target group, chances are none of them show up on your radar.

The market leader and challenger roles are well documented, for example in *Eating the big Fish* (Morgan 2009) and you'll find this dynamic as the main rule of most categories. However, generic categories where the brands' offerings and promises are more or less identical do exist. In such cases, competition is usually more about price than the strengths of the brand, and the key to success is cost efficiency across the value chain more than brand building.

In some categories, a small number of providers have all but split the market between them. Brands in these categories are particularly vulnerable in times of technological turmoil. New, innovative brands that challenge the hegemony of the incumbents can attract quite a following. It's hard enough to be a market leader, or a challenger for that matter, in a category going through a technological shift. But it is even harder in a category where brands have no higher ambition than maintaining existing price points and distribution models.

However, I have worked with brands where neither the category market leader, nor the challenger role has seemed appropriate. These are brands that don't view the competitive arena as a battle between itself and a given competitor. In these cases, we may be looking at a pioneer role. The pioneer role is different from the others in that it does not compete with known players on predefined selection criteria in a familiar arena, but rather challenges the entire category

Roles

Market Leader

Builds the category and sets the rules

Challenger

A clear alternative to the market leader

Pioneer

Challenges the entire category

and all its conventions by bringing something new to the table. We will now look at each of the three roles in some detail, considering their strengths and weaknesses and learning more about how each of them court favour with the people.

The market leader

The market leader has the greatest market share and is the most profitable brand in the category. The market leader's differentiated position will often be based on taking ownership of the customers' most important selection criterion. The market leader has the resources and market insight to allow it to define the rules to compete by and shape the market's category expectations. An effective market leader's most important job is establishing the category in people's minds and continuing to develop it. However, this is also a great opportunity to craft the brand's positioning, its identity, messaging and choice of communication channels with a great degree of freedom.

As the market leader tends to be the brand that established the category in people's minds, the marked leader brands are often very closely associated with the category. The verb "google" has become synonymous with searching the Internet for information, although Google was far from the first search engine on the market.

When Tesla launched its Roadster in 2008, it shook the electric car industry. Both by introducing a new criterion entirely – a sexy electric car, who knew! – and by taking ownership of the most important criterion, namely distance. In terms of reach, the Tesla cars outperformed all other electric cars by far and set a new standard to beat.

As mentioned, the market leader is not necessarily the first brand to market. In fact, Netscape was the first mainstream search engine. And Reva in India, Neighbourhood Electric Vehicle (NEV) in the United States and Think in Europe already had cars in the market long before Tesla existed. Both Samsung and Google, and the Kickstarter funded Pebble, had fully fledged smart watches long before Apple Watch. However, it's the first brand to reach a critical mass of people's minds that tends to win the category and also dominate it over time.

The market leader's most important job

It falls to the market leader to lead the way, ploughing the road as it were for other brands. The market leader has the resources to invest in keeping the category vital and visible. The market leader stands to gain the most as the category grows. Baking the cake bigger and helping itself to the largest piece of it, is a greater opportunity for continued growth than fighting with competitors for a share of a smaller cake.

The market leader is like a category ambassador, taking every opportunity to speak enthusiastically on behalf of it (bragging about yourself when everybody knows you're the biggest and best is so unbecoming). The market leader has power, but should use it wisely. It will defend its position and grab market share where it can, but the market leader should also recognise its competitors for what they are; helpers in the effort to maintain people's interest in the category, and keeping the market leader on its toes at the same time.

The market leader has the largest customer base; their customers usually shop more or more often than their competitors' customers do. Thus, the market leader has greater opportunity for dialogue with a greater number of people and can build more relationships than any other player in its market.

When the market leader falls asleep at the wheel

A dedicated market leader will often be able to show high scores for customer satisfaction. As long as the market leader continues to do its job well, it's almost impossible to usurp its position. As a rule, the greater the market leader's market share, the less effort it takes to grow further. Smaller players would have to invest manifold what the market leader does to achieve similar visibility and opportunity to grow their business.

However, a market leader tough enough to challenge and disrupt its own technologies and business models is a rare thing to behold. As the story goes, Kodak actually developed a digital camera. But the company powers that be felt confident people would always want physical prints and negatives of their pictures, so the market for digital solutions would be negligible.

When a market leader falls asleep at the wheel, or makes itself unpopular through excessive and/or unethical use of its powers, it becomes hard to maintain market leadership. In this type of situation, people are more likely to be tempted by competing offers. A market leader can never allow itself to become complacent, even if seemingly far ahead in the race. Market leaders must stay hungry, watch closely for disruptive innovations in the market and take it upon themselves to be innovators. Leading businesses keep their ears to the ground; watch out for trends and what's happening in the market with the aim of introducing new features, products or services when the market has reached the right level of maturity. New market introductions may be the result of in-house innovations, new alliances or the acquisition of innovative businesses.

This is why Unilever acquired Ben & Jerry's, Google acquired YouTube, and Facebook acquired Instagram. Amazon developed Alexa and Tesla is developing self driving capability technology for its electric cars.

The market leader role comes with a set of norms and expectations that businesses should also take into consideration in their brand building efforts.

The Challenger

A challenger's role is to be a clear alternative to the market leader. The relative strengths of the market leader and the challenger will influence how the challenger acts out its challenge to the market leader, but as a general rule the challenger personality tends to be bolder, louder and keener than that of a market leader.

While the market leader wants to be the best option for the greatest number of people, the challenger may target a smaller but more specific group of potential customers, may represent a different set of values or claim to have a different reason to exist or to believe in something that is different from the belief system of the market leader brand. The challenger's job is not to be relevant to everybody, but to focus all its efforts on being great at whatever it is it wants to be known for. And while a market leader is barred by convention from boasting about its own excellence, no such restrictions exist for the challenger. People generally find it perfectly acceptable, even charming, when challengers speak enthusiastically about themselves.

Benefits of surfing in the leader's wake

Most strategists will agree that positioning a brand or creating a strategy for a business without knowing the competition is impossible. For challenger brands in particular, the strategy must take the market leader's strengths and brand position as their starting point.

Nevertheless, the challenger enjoys a greater degree of freedom than the market leader, both with regard to defining the brand identity and carving out its niche in the competitive arena. One of the challenger's benefits is that it does not have to do the heavy lifting of promoting the category. Rather, the challenger can piggyback on the work done by the market leader on behalf of the entire category, and instead focus its resources on presenting itself as an alternative to the number one brand, both when it comes to differentiation and identity.

Also, the challenger can more easily make use of the increasingly valuable currency of empathy. Traditionally, the market leader's most valuable currency has been 'safe', and the value of safe is in sharp decline in our day and age where quality and price are becoming ever more transparent and switching costs minimal. So, the path to choosing a challenger brand that people like – perhaps for no other reason than everybody roots for the underdog – becomes very short indeed. The most famous challenger slogan may be Avis' *We try harder*! (and that's exactly what people like about challengers).

A category without a clear challenger brand tends to be a little bland, the players in it not very well differentiated and usually not characterized by innovation. There's no incentive to invest in innovation where no competition is looming, or if the battle for market share is fought primarily through price and distribution power. Nor does this this kind of battle give the customers any reason to engage. This may well be a comfortable scenario in a stable marked, but it does leave the incumbent players vulnerable to emerging innovators.

In contrast, categories where one brand steps up to take the challenger role are characterized by positive energy that benefits both the market leader and the challenger. Samsung was a well-known Asian affordable electronics brand, but then it decided to take on Apple and the iPhone as a challenger in the smartphone category. Samsung's clear challenger position made the brand more visible in this space and allowed the brand to stand out and grab market share from less visible competitor brands.

Attacking the market leader's strengths

One might think that the best positioning for a challenger brand is to be strong where the market leader is weak. However, that may turn out to be a short term solution. A market leader will usually have the time and resources to fix a specific weakness when challenged. The most dangerous challengers position themselves in such a way as to turn the market leader's strengths against them.

If, for example, the market leader brand represents the value 'safe', the challenger can reposition the market leader as 'boring'. For this reason, challenger identities tend to be crafted in clear contrast to the market leader's brand identity.

The battle of David and Goliath is the classic narrative of this kind, and challengers will often cast themselves as the little hero standing up to the seemingly invincible giant. However, this is far from the only way the challenger market leader dynamic can play out. In the book *Overthrow* (Morgan and Holden 2012) you will find ten different challenger scripts describing different approaches to positioning a challenger brand. One example is the democratizer script, where the strategy is to take something exclusive and available only to the few, and make it available to the general masses. The Spanish brand Zara is a good example of a democratizer. It will have its versions of designer dresses on hangers in its shops around the world, only weeks after we saw the originals on the catwalks, at a price many more of us can afford.

The scripts in *Overthrow* are not step-by-step playbooks to success, but they illustrate well how the key to forming your brand's challenger identity must be found through analysis of the competitive arena. It's a good idea to learn from the experience of others and in this book, you'll find great examples of market leaders and challengers that compete in a way that brings out the best in both.

The pioneer

The market leader and challenger dynamic has been well documented and described over time. However, a third role is emerging, which is useful to understand as a separate role – namely the pioneer brand.

What defines a pioneer, first and foremost, is that the brand is powered by passion for an idea, a worldview or values that it sets higher than anything happening in the traditional competitive arena in the battle for market share. The pioneer will clearly and enthusiastically advocate its idea and actively recruit people to its way of seeing things.

We took our skills from the entertainment industry and translated them to work in airlines

Sir Richard Branson

The Telegraph, 2014

In the book *Eating the big fish* (2009) Adam Morgan describes an attitude he calls intelligently naïve. The intelligently naïve pioneer asks why are things like *that*, why can't they be like *this*? The pioneer is also less concerned with the battle taking place in the category's competitive arena, focusing instead on doing its own thing in its own way.

Rather than challenge a specific market leader, the pioneer challenges the entire category. Pioneers emerge on the scene with plenty of enthusiasm and very little respect for the category rules. By questioning norms and assumptions, the pioneer can bring something new and fresh to the market. In contrast to the market leader and challenger who position themselves according to the established selection criteria of the category, the pioneer tends to introduce new criteria, a new price point, a new mode of distribution, business model, a new kind of customer relationship or attitude that explains and justifies its behaviour in the market.

When Apple launched its first iPhone it was introduced as a small, yet fully functional computer that – by the way – was also a phone. In reality, the iPhone competed with all the other products in the mobile phone category, redefining it and shifting positions for all other players in the category.

Pioneer behaviour

It's in the pioneer's nature to defy boundaries, but to the extent that it is possible to describe a typical pioneer, it's perhaps best done by looking at typical pioneer behaviour. Successful pioneers tend to have these things in common:
- They have an idea that is greater than their business idea.
- They speak to friends and fans, not so much consumers, target groups or the general public as such.

- They continue to find new ways to reinvent their category and strengthen the brand's relationship with friends.
- They are happy to collaborate with like-minded brands to further a common cause.

Some describe the pioneer as a kind of challenger, others claim it's a market leader in the making. Considering the current speed of innovation and change, it's fair to ask whether being a pioneer is more about a specific attitude than a specific role in the market. Today, all players – even market leaders – can and sometimes must assume the pioneer role to drive through fundamental changes in their category. Either way, the pioneer is ambiguous and tricky to pin down in that it challenges the traditional market leader challenger dynamic.

Three potential pioneer routes

A pioneer can bring about a shift in an existing category by introducing a substitute. When the category settles again after the disruption, the previous category owner will be gone or marginalized and the pioneer's way of seeing things dominates. When this happens, the pioneer inherits the role and responsibilities of the former market leader. However, it's crucial for the pioneer to remain exactly that at heart, at least if it wants to keep its friends and fans happy. Again, it can be useful to look to Apple's entry onto the smartphone arena, a pioneer that brought about a shift in a category it quickly came to dominate.

Another pioneer option is to establish a clear sub category. Southwest Airlines is an example of a pioneer that shifted the entire airline industry towards a much lower price point by redefining the selection criteria in the category. Comfort and service criteria were simply replaced by the price criterion and the driving principle of making the fares a cheap as possible. And that's how Southwest Airlines in the US, and Ryanair in Europe came to dominate a new sub category, namely the low cost airline category. Similarly, one might view Airbnb as the de facto market leader in a new hospitality sub category.

However, pioneers don't always turn into new market leaders or establish new sub categories. Many pioneers choose a third path, selecting to remain in that unique position over time, largely unaffected by the battles between the established players in a category's competitive arena. Instead they choose to be happy with a smaller yet sufficient number of dedicated patrons. Toms (formerly Toms Shoes) is an example of this type of pioneer, combining fashion with aid under its *One for One* slogan. For each pair of shoes sold, the company will donate a pair to someone who needs it. Customers can easily love the company's mission as much as the shoes they buy. Lately Toms has extended this strategy beyond footwear, entering other markets such as eyewear, rucksacks and water. Notice how Toms' brand extensions did not happen by expanding to categories on the fringes of shoes, but focused instead on categories where its one for one strategy makes the most sense. Virgin is another example of a brand that has lived by its own rules, for example what an airline can and should be, competing well as a pioneer alternative in the various categories it has chosen to take on.

What determines a brand's role?

For many brands, it's easy to point out what role they play in a category. Sometimes, which brands play which part is well established and well known in the businesses themselves and in the market. For other brands, the role is much more dynamic and may change in accordance with a brand's rise and/or fall in a category. Imagine for example what happens when the market leader of a sub category decides to challenge the market leader of the main category. Consider also the changes taking place within a category characterized by frequent acquisitions, introduction of disruptive technologies or fundamental shifts in its regulatory framework – ideal conditions for innovators looking to move in on "fat and lazy" incumbent market leaders. It will, for example, be interesting to see which brands emerge to take advantage of the current lack of trust in the banking category in general, particularly among young people.

Better to reign in Hell than serve in Heaven?
The first step towards understanding the roles in a category is to perform a competitor analysis. The analysis should make clear the positioning of the various players and which brands play which role in the market. One way to do this is to create a visual category map, placing the different competitors in relation to each other.

When you have your visual map of the category, you can start analysing the communication going on within it. What are the different brands' key messages? What promises do they make? How do they talk about themselves when talking to the customers? Next, you can see if you can discover parallels in other markets and/or in similar categories. This gives us a rough overview of the competitive landscape and an understanding of which brands are cast in which roles.

Why is this important? Because categories are continuously changing, and shifts within a category impact how the brands in it play out their roles. Today, the car category is enormous, but it wasn't always so. At the time when Henry Ford set up his assembly lines and invented industrial car manufacture, the car category was almost a category of one, the T-Ford. Since then, the category has been inundated with cars targeted at specific user groups, designed to cover a range of functional requirements or to suit various situations. When a category balloons like this, and it becomes difficult to keep track of all the alternatives in it, the category tends to split into more manageable chunks in the form of sub categories.

Your brand's identity also plays a part in determining how its role is performed. The brand identity derives from the brand's behaviour, a sum of all the strategic choices made about how the brand should act in order to secure its position in the market. It's useful to envisage the brand as if it were a person, assigning it human traits and properties. Having defined these aspects of your brand's identity will help ensure that it plays out its role in the category well and develops a consistent brand identity at the same time.

In the chapters about archetypes and identity we will look more closely at how to build a compelling brand identity that really helps you stand out from the crowd.

We are now at the point in the book where we have looked at defining a brand's category and role, so you are already well on your way towards positioning it. However, the positioning part of your brand platform isn't done until you have also decided how to differentiate it clearly from its competitors.

Chapter 4

Differentiation – deserving a place in people's minds

This chapter on differentiation is most of all about prioritisation. When we prefer some brands over others, we do so for a reason. There are reasons why some brands stand out more clearly than other brands in a category. In this chapter, we will sort through some of these reasons and tidy up the criteria behind our brand selection choices. Organising and prioritising these criteria is a useful exercise that raises the level of awareness about what makes a brand unique. Thus, understanding differentiation helps anyone who communicates, acts or innovates on behalf of a brand to understand which criteria to focus on and in what way.

What exactly do you think differentiates a Snickers from a Mars bar? Really? What makes you select one and not the other?

Is it the situation you're in? Who you are with, how much you are going to eat, price, taste, the peanuts or that Joan Collins ad? If you were tasked with defining the difference between the two in a way that's helpful to packaging designers, website creators or campaign managers, what would you say? Even when we know the products well, this is not an easy exercise. Successful and lasting differentiation is the result of a series of choices that all together build preferences over time.

On the one hand, differentiation sounds solid, business-y and strategy-ish, unlike terms such as concept, idea or reputation – to name but a few. However, the term differentiation is often used with no clear notion of what is to be differentiated from what or whether we are talking about a brand's category, product, personality or communication.

Brand strategy and business strategy is not the same thing, but both disciplines are about choosing direction. For the business and the brand alike, the purpose of strategic positioning is to establish lasting competitive advantages by protecting and strengthening that which is distinctly different from the competition. Different in this context means doing other things than your competitors do, or doing the same things in different ways.

So, differentiation is achieved through a series of choices and prioritisations in line with your chosen brand position. Most decisions viewed in isolation can be copied quite easily, but a continuous flow of decisions made to strengthen its strategic position across an entire organisation is much harder to copy. In principle, all furniture retailers can sell flat packed bookshelves, serve meatballs in their cafeterias and have ballrooms for children to play in while parents shop, but that doesn't make them IKEA.

Differentiation concerns both the positioning of your business in the physical competitive arena and the positioning of your brand in people's minds. Of course, the two are connected. Still, it's even harder to find a vacant spot in people's minds than out there in the real world, so when it comes to branding you have to be very disciplined when selecting the number of criteria to compete on and make sure you are very, very clear where you stand on these.

The differentiation rocket

The differentiation rocket is a useful tool to get this job done. The rocket metaphor is based on the work of Keller & Tybouts (2002) and the well established separation between points of parity (where a brand has to be on a par with the competition), points of differentiation (which are the criteria where a brand wants to stand out as better than the competition), and finally, the unique selling proposition (the criterion or promise a brand wants to own outright). Think back to the chocolates at the beginning of this chapter. Both chocolates must be sweet and in that they are quite similar. However, only one of them contains peanuts, which is a physical differentiation factor. While the Mars bar is closely associated with children, play and fun times, Snickers is the meal you crave when you're "hangry".

When we're working with differentiation, the discussion sometimes gets side-tracked, becoming a discussion about how some things are more important than others. While this is true, the relative importance of everything you do to win in the market is not really the issue at hand. What we want to stay focused on is defining as clearly as possible what we aim to build in people's minds.

It takes an awful lot to create a great product, a successful service, a meaningful community or a profitable business, and

Differentiation Rocket

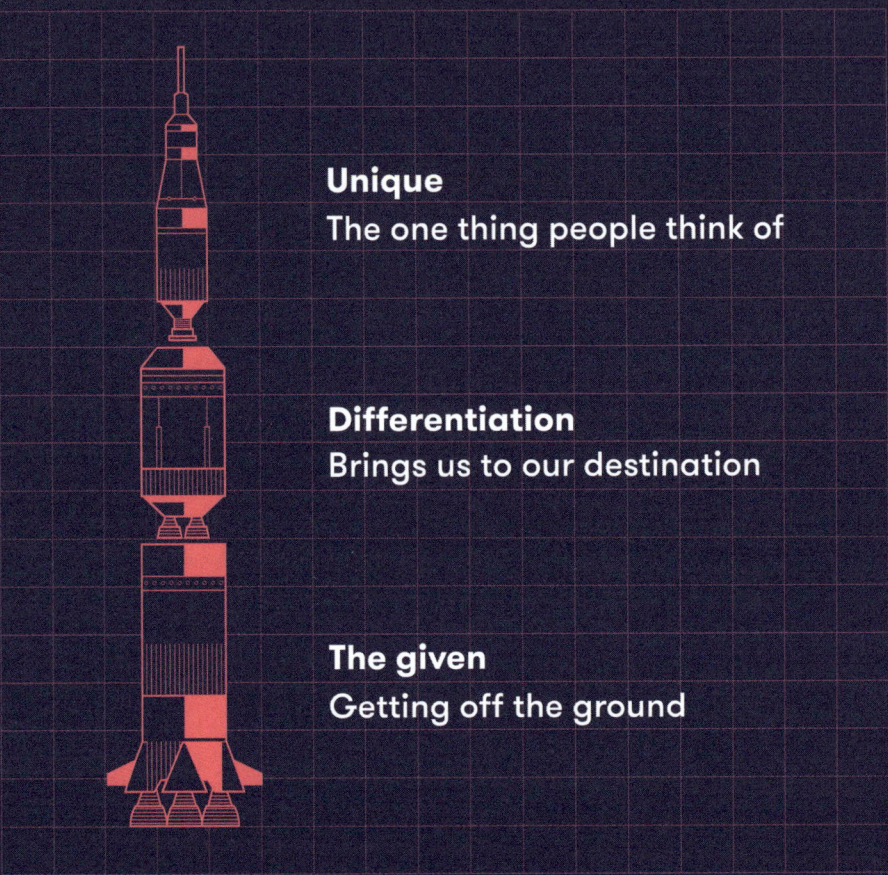

Unique
The one thing people think of

Differentiation
Brings us to our destination

The given
Getting off the ground

Tag along on this little rocket analogy

To understand this model more easily, please bear with me on this rocket analogy. After years of hard work, NASA sent the Curiosity rover on its way towards Mars. Just getting the spaceship off the ground required enormous resources and burned about half the fuel of the entire mission.

Next followed a long journey transporting the rover to the red planet. What we remember, however, are the images from the little rover's exploration of Mars' surface. It's the same way with branding. We spend huge amounts of time and effort to plant a very small message in people's minds.

all the things it takes are dreadfully important. Companies and organisations are usually more than keen to tell us about all the important things they are doing, but most of their efforts amount to the equivalent of getting the rocket off the ground. Unfortunately, not many people care. Talking about all the things you do well is simply a way of creating noise that makes it harder for your brand to be heard. The thing you really want to be known for is drowned out by everything else. What you want to get out of your work with the differentiation rocket is to identify exactly what it is that makes your brand unique and make sure that's what stands out by reducing the noise of all the other important things you feel like talking about.

First what, then how

There are two things you need to get your head around before you're in a position to define your brand's differentiation clearly. Firstly, what are the differentiation criteria, and secondly, how will your brand deliver on them. Take something simple, such as price, for example. Sometimes price is irrelevant as a selection criterion. Again, the chocolates are a case in point. I'll bet you don't know how much more or less you pay for a Snickers compared to a Mars bar.

However, in categories where price is relevant to the brand, it's not only whether your price is higher or lower than the competition that impacts your brand. In fact, everything around your price point policy will influence people's perception of your brand, such as number of models and their price range (think Tesla compared to Audi), how much the prices fluctuate over time (the electronics retail chains and the price of televisions) or the business model itself (streaming versus owning).

Differentiation is a moving target

The digital shift has brought new instabilities, which makes it more difficult to create and maintain solid positions. New kinds of competitors arrive on the scene seemingly overnight, business models are challenged in radical ways and entire industries are split or merged, while trends, values and people's perceptions of what's hot or not changes constantly. Consequently, the differentiating criteria are also changing constantly, and the same must go for a brand's choice in how to deliver on each criterion. Brands do well to remember that all the little decisions should be in line with the greater brand strategy of making sure each of the decisions that seem trivial in isolation play their part in building a clear, coherent and strong brand. The same goes for decisions that require your organisation to pull together across its various functions. It's more effective if product development and HR alike are familiar with the brand's differentiation strategy and use it to guide their decision-making. How – if at all – does a product development decision to eliminate all use of palm oil impact a brand? Or what is the impact to the brand when an organisation chooses to implement really good professional development programmes for its staff? It should be possible to revisit the entire system of criteria, and your brand's responses to the criteria, at any time to monitor the system's relevance, that your choices actually reinforce each other and continue to strengthen your brand.

The differentiation rocket will be even more useful to you, if you assign each of the three levels a headline that captures what your brand's choices on each level aim to achieve. That way, you make sure that you're not only mapping out the criteria your brand needs to meet, compete on and own, but explicitly stating what the result of each of the choices should be. Then, you'll be clear on what your real world choices should help build in people's minds.

These objectives will make it easier to see the entire system of differentiating criteria and your brand's responses to each as an integrated whole. At the same time, you'll also be able to keep editing the system in accordance with changes happening in your competitive arena, without having to start from scratch every time.

Just like our rocket, your differentiation system has three levels, one for the goes-without-saying criteria, one for the differentiating criteria and one for what makes your brand unique.

Getting off the ground
– the goes-without-saying criteria

On this level, you will find the basic criteria of the category; what your brand needs to deliver on to even be a selectable alternative. In other words, it's what you need to have to get off the ground. While these criteria are fundamental to competing in the category, they are not necessarily the kind of criteria potential customers actively evaluate when considering the options available to them.

As mentioned above, we're not looking for an exhaustive list of everything a brand needs to do to be a category player in the real world. That would be one long list indeed. What we are looking to create is a list of criteria that are *perceived* as fundamental when people look at a category and which brands belong to it so that we can differentiate our brand from the others on those criteria. The relevance of a criterion, such as price for example, will vary from category to category. While price may not be a criterion you differentiate your chocolate bar choices on, it may be highly relevant to streaming services for films and TV-shows.

Some criteria have become more important over the past few years, for example how organisations take corporate social responsibility and related factors like sustainability and taking a stand on social issues. It's still possible for organisations in industries that have neglected this area in the past to build attractive differentiation around its corporate social responsibility efforts. However, in category after category, people expect no less and will not reward brands for being ethical and sustainable – it goes without saying and belongs to the bottom level of the rocket. Even so, brands still have to respond to this expectation by actively choosing *how* to go about taking social responsibility.

The rule of thumb for the bottom level of the rocket is as follows: If a given criterion is not perceived as fulfilled, potential customers will not consider your brand a relevant option in the category. Any existing customer will replace your brand with a brand that does fulfil it at the first opportunity. An example is one click shopping. After Amazon replaced the (up until then) cumbersome process of online checkout, with it's one click to buy, we simply didn't accept longwinded online shopping experiences anymore. What was initially a competitive advantage for Amazon, was adopted by other online retailers as a necessary measure to stay in the game. *How* they choose to simplify the checkout process varies.

Some refer to these kinds of selection criteria as hygiene factors, meaning something you don't even notice as long as it's taken care of, but that creates disappointment and frustration when not. If you visit the ladies or gents of a restaurant and find that there is toilet paper available, it's unlikely that you will be impressed and become a loyal patron of the establishment in gratitude. Should you visit the same bathroom and find no paper when you need it – disaster!

And that's the way it is with these goes-without-saying criteria. They are critically important, but not critically important to talk about, unless you are fighting to establish your brand as a legitimate alternative in the category at all.

Category criteria

The headline of this goes-without-saying level will typically be tied to the category in the manner of: to compete in the xyz-category, we must meet the following criteria. As mentioned in the chapter about roles, the market leader will often be in a position to define what these criteria are. That in turn gives the market leader the privilege not only to define the criteria, but also to go first when it comes to deciding how to fulfil each.

Starbucks defined its coffee shops as not exactly home, not quite work, but as a "third space" where you can hang out comfortably as long as you like. Providing this type of environment has become a coffee shop category criterion. Starbucks also defined, and named, the different sizes of its beverages and gave new names to various coffee based beverages, which other coffee shops have to provide their own versions of to compete in the same category. Similarly, Maldon salt defined that gourmet salt comes in crystals, so if you want to compete in the gourmet salt category you better position your salt crystals as a clearly differentiated alternative to Maldon, but crystals nevertheless.

We live in turbulent times and it's important for brands to follow even the category defining criteria closely. Before you know it, an innovative player (taking a pioneer role) may introduce new criteria or reshuffle the list of criteria, even if the criteria for being a viable option in the category has been stable in the past. Let the rise of streaming services and the emergence of sharing economy alternatives that impact category after category be a word of warning to traditional providers that fail to pay attention as the world changes around them.

Choosing to compete in a new category can infuse an organisation with a tremendous amount of energy. Brands, or organisations looking to build brands that are not yet firmly positioned in a clear category can find inspiration as well as direction at this level of the rocket. An example is cities. Some cities that for historical or other reasons aren't clearly positioned in our minds, benefit greatly from defining a clearer category and its differentiation within it. As a result, the city can more easily attract tourists, events, investment and even new inhabitants. Look at what happened when Glasgow changed its category from tired, rusty, industrial city of dodgy reputation to European cultural city in 1990. By competing as a cultural city, rather than the largest city of Scotland, a whole new set of category attributes and properties applied, and the same goes for the list of selection criteria. Now, Glasgow could focus on creating expectations as to what kind of cultural city it was going to be and how to communicate what made Glasgow a unique cultural city to the groups that the city wanted to attract. The city of Oslo is in the process of going through a similar exercise as I write this. Rather than competing as the third largest Scandinavian capital, Oslo will compete in the compact city stage category – differentiated by its opportunities for adventure and as one of the very few cities in Europe with a growing population of young people. As such it made sense to decline a bid for the 2022 winter Olympics, but enthusiastically host the X-games in 2016.

Towards your destination
– differentiating criteria

On this level, you find the criteria that potential customers evaluate actively and perceive as most important when comparing brands in a category. Sometimes, the list of criteria to be fulfilled by all brands in the category can seem quite fixed even on this level. However, it is becoming less common to see competitors locked in what then becomes a kind of benchmarking battle. When every player competes with everyone else on all the criteria, rather than make strategic choices about where exactly to excel, everyone loses. Working this level of the rocket is most useful when you populate it with the criteria you *choose* to compete on and define *how* your brand fulfils these compared to the competition.

Differentiating criteria can be about something fairly concrete such as functionality (digital services), design (products), price (retail chain) or travel time (airline), but it's also useful to include criteria that play a role in strengthening the relationship with your customers specifically.

On this level, it's not unusual for the chosen criteria, as well as how your brand deals with them, to be the ones that enable the brand to play out its role in the category. Is the market leader an active innovator in its category? Is the challenger a clear alternative to the market leader by responding differently to the criteria set by the market leader? Has the challenger or pioneer introduced a whole new set of criteria?

Learning from the best
When working with this level of the rocket, it's useful to look to successful brands that have a similar role to your brand, only in other categories. What is it these brands do to make people

want to connect, and how do they successfully motivate people to advocate for the brand? Perhaps you can be inspired by measures taken by other market leaders to drive innovation on behalf of an entire category (such as the opulent Victoria's Secret shows aired on TV, or GE's Open Innovation Manifesto) or you can allow yourself to learn from how other challengers succeed in becoming a clear alternative to the market leaders through the choices and actions that characterize their particular kind of challenger behaviour (such as the way Pepsi, Samsung and Burger King like to poke fun at their somewhat more sanctimonious competitors). Observe also how pioneers come in and reshuffle all the selection criteria in category after category (Foodora is neither restaurant nor a traditional take-away brand, but rather a way to eat out even if you'd like to stay home. Faced with the super quick Foodora cyclists that pick up meals from a wide range of restaurants and bring them to people's homes, restaurants and take away restaurants alike have to think about the way they fulfil selection criteria such as quality and availability all over again.)

On this level, it's very important to be specific about how your brand is different from its competitors, and exactly what it is you do that is different. For example, Apple is the brand for ground-breaking technology and uncompromising simplicity of design, whereas the Android brands are positioned in opposition to Apple's proprietary standards by offering a greater degree of choice and variety.

This will not be an exercise you can do once and be done – which criteria are considered differentiating changes over time. Think back to when touch screens first entered the smartphone arena, triggering many a purchasing decision. Today, you'd be hard pressed to find a smartphone without a large, high definition, crisp colour touch screen. Consequently, the touchscreen criterion no longer has the same potential for differentiation and has moved down to the rocket's bottom level – *goes-without-saying*.

Touchdown – where your brand is unique

In *The Immutable Laws of Marketing* (1994) Reiss and Trout claimed that the best a brand can hope for is to own a word, a promise or concept in people's minds. This word, promise or concept is placed right at the very top of the rocket – it designates that one thing that makes your brand unique in its category.

The goal is that when put together, all the criteria you choose and the way you choose to fulfil them lead to your brand standing out as a clear alternative, and ideally as unique. The word you place at the rocket's tip cannot do this job by itself, so it's important for all the levels of the rocket to work together as a whole. Each level of the rocket supports and builds up under whatever it is you aim for your brand to own in people's minds; that word, promise or concept you have placed at its top.

According to current brand strategy thinking, the relationship between the brand and its customers/market is considered much more valuable than a unique selling proposition as such. Nevertheless, if your brand achieves clear ownership of, or a strong association with, a criterion or something the market finds attractive, that's still a useful platform on which to build those relationships.

We'll get back to how to go about making such a criterion stand out clearly in people's minds, but before moving on it's worth reiterating – remember that we are looking for two things here: to define both the criteria themselves on each level of the rocket and how your brand chooses to fulfil them.

Some brands own a patent or have properties that are impossible to copy. For everyone else, brands are built through how they fulfil all the selection criteria and it's the sum of all these how-choices that gives credibility to the top of your rocket. Great brands use the little things as opportunities to remind people why they want to connect and stay connected to it. Such as when Innocent included the following in its list of ingredients on the juice bottle: 9 crushed raspberries, a chunk of mashed banana and some lovely honey" (Innocent, 2007).

When all the levels of the rocket play together, it gives you a recipe of the things you'll want to do, and how you have chosen to do them. The result is a brand that stands for something unique in people's minds and motivates the behaviours we aim for.

One example: On the bottom level of the rocket, the pioneer brand Virgin Atlantic needed to cover all the criteria for what it takes to be transatlantic airline (its category): the flights, its price point, the experience, loyalty programmes and so on. The brand is differentiated from the competition in the category by its promise that air travel – and running an airline – is fun. So, in the middle of the rocket you will find all the things this airline does differently, its pioneer attitude and entertainment industry legacy; rock and roll, fun and games and various forms of artist audience interactions. At the very top of Virgin Atlantic's rocket you'll find its unique personality. It challenges convention with its *Flying in the face* of ordinary slogan, and challenges everything that is dull in the airline industry by promising to be *a welcome splash of red in a weary sea of grey*. However, while its personality permeates everything the airline does, real choices are made about where exactly to concentrate its brand building measures, because not absolutely everything can be fun, fun, fun. That would be exhausting for its customers and very expensive for the brand to sustain. Advertising and social media efforts are important, but the services provided inside the cabin and on the ground, uniforms, security demonstrations, launches of new routes and planes and similar, are at least equally important. The way Virgin Atlantic goes about these things are consistently more tongue in cheek, sexier and more entertaining than anyone else's and things happen at Virgin Atlantic that happen nowhere else. This way, Virgin Atlantic has built a brand that means something to people whether they are die hard fans, loyal when they can afford to be, simply dream of flying Upper Class or just really like the brand even if they have not experienced it first hand – yet.

Differentiation and role

What is most attractive for a brand to own depends to a large extent on its role in the market. Market leader and challenger scripts alike, that is, our expectations to each role, are very real in people's minds. This is helpful to remember as role awareness can help you approach the task of differentiation more efficiently. As mentioned earlier in this book, ownership of the most important criterion tends to belong to the market leader. The challenger should identify and compete on the second most important criterion, which will very often, but not always, be price.

As a fullback at the University of Maryland, Kevin Plank got tired of having to change out of the sweat-soaked T-shirts worn under his jersey. He noticed, however, that his compression shorts worn during practice stayed dry. And that was the beginning of the American sports apparel brand Under Armour (Under Armour 2017). Under Armour is challenging Nike's *Just do it* with a forceful *I will what I want*, celebrating the will to push boundaries and eliminate all that stands in the way of training really hard, whether those impediments be bouncy bits (I will not

7 kinds

According to Kapferer (2012) there are seven different routes to defining something unique to take ownership of in your category. These seven approaches are useful to look at when you're working to identify which criteria might be relevant and sort through the prioritisation of the criteria that are.

1. A differentiating attribute. The Dove bar of soap contains moisturizing cream. Domino's has a pizza delivery guarantee.

2. An objective benefit. Duracell batteries last longer. There's no deeper clean then Listerine.

3. A subjective benefit. Ray-Bans are never wrong. Nespresso caters to sophisticated tastes.

4. An aspect of the brand's personality. Joe & the Juice flirts with everyone. Jack Daniel's whisky is masculine and down to earth.

5. The realm of the imaginary or an image we have of a way of life. Citizen M caters to a modern mobile lifestyle, Ben & Jerry's invokes a happy, organic, Vermont hippie culture.

6. A reflection of a consumer type. Nike is for winners. Red Bull is for thrill seekers.

7. Deep values or a mission. Patagonia wants us to consume responsively. Procter & Gamble is the proud sponsor of moms.

be unsupported) or sweaty t-shirts (I will not be uncomfortable). While Nike's promise of performance enhancement starts from the shoe up, Under Armour works from the skin out. Nike speaks to you as an athlete, Under Armour sees you working out.

Working the differentiation rocket

When making use of the rocket analogy, as we work to define a differentiated position for a brand, the objective is always to discover the main criteria brands compete on and decide how to fulfil each of them. Typically, just like in any strategy process, the greatest difficulty is finding a way to view your brand as if from outside, like any other player in the competitive arena. It's far too easy to get stuck in one's regular inside out perspective, taking the organisation's strengths – of which it may be rightly proud – as the starting point for the differentiation process. The current business strategy paradigm, the resource based view, takes as its starting point the business' unique set of resources. And it makes a lot of sense to argue that a brand's differentiation must be based on what the business can actually deliver to have any kind of credibility. However, that's not the objective of the rocket exercise. We use it to map out a differentiation that is attractive in the category, relevant to customers, available in the competitive arena and credible for the brand to take ownership of – all viewed from the perspective of potential customers or users. It happens way too often that businesses try to build brands on strengths that unfortunately others have already taken firm ownership of, or that even if it is available and credible for the brand to own, simply isn't important enough in the category to be a criterion you can compete on to win market share.

As a rule of thumb, what's at the top of the rocket is closely tied to the category (for attractiveness and relevance) and the role your brand plays in it (for availability and credibility). At its best, this exercise will tell you an awful lot about how you should build your brand. While the overall objective is to establish your brand in the minds of people, it must be done in a way that takes into consideration what your organisation is made of and the things that are important to your company culture.

Businesses that don't have a well considered position on their own identity and differentiation often have a bit of a Eureka moment during the process of sorting through the criteria and prioritising them according to the rocket's logic. Some realise that there is nothing unique about what they would place at the top, whereas others find that people don't really care about the thing they place at the top, even if it's utterly unique. Let's imagine a Swiss watch manufacturer that has successfully focused on the accuracy of its timepieces in the past. Then comes a wide variety of digital gadgets that show the time with at least the same accuracy, shifting the whole timepiece category in their wake. Perhaps the Swiss manufacturer should now focus on criteria that have previously belonged to jewellery categories, now that the relevance of the beauty, luxury or design of its watches far surpasses that of the accuracy criterion.

Discovering the criteria

Start by a thorough messaging analysis to discover which criteria are most relevant to the positioning of your brand. Go through internal documents, customer satisfaction surveys, competitor analysis of relevant players in your category and similar categories. Which are the most important criteria in the category? What do people *really* think and what do they *really* care about? Where do the findings from strategy documents and customer and/or user surveys and competitors' communication converge? The most useful list of relevant criteria for your brand's differentiated position comes from looking at differentiation both as your customers would see it, and from an understanding of the dynamics of your category.

Which criteria are your competitors fighting over?

Having discovered a long list of selection criteria in your category, the time has come for sorting them into the differentiation rocket. You should populate the bottom and middle levels of the rocket in such a way that they support and reinforce whatever you have placed at the rocket's top, the thing that makes your brand unique. These are questions to consider as you work:

- What do you have to fulfil not to be rejected? Are the criteria historically determined and will they remain relevant beyond the digital shift? Can you discover categories that are moving in on your category, that perhaps have a different set of attributes, promises or values that threaten to make your entire category less attractive?
- What do people associate with your brand? Can you discover elements that are less relevant now that people's willingness to bond with your brand is so much more valuable than being associated with instrumental promises? Have you lost or forgotten important legacy from your brand's early days as a result of your business growing or as your industry has matured?
- Who would you say people bond with – your product/service or the business that provides it? Do you think that will continue to be the case, or can you discover trends that may affect this connection?
- What can you claim, or what do you aim to claim ownership of in your category? Is it attractive, relevant, available and credible both now and in the future? Is there any goal or objective in particular that would energize and motivate your organisation? Can you claim any kind of differentiation

that is built into your business model, or that's difficult to copy because it touches so many parts of your value chain or network? Is your differentiation in line with the culture and values of your organisation?

Start at the bottom and when you are done with this level, move up to the middle. Look carefully at the criteria where brands seem to make different choices that set them apart from each other, as these are criteria you'll most likely want to include here.

Alternatively, you can approach this exercise by taking your brand's relationship to its market, customers and/or its users as your starting point. What do other brands – perhaps in unrelated categories – do to build the kinds of relationships you're looking to build for your brand? If you think this is the way forward for you, then populate the goes-without-saying level with the things it takes to win customers purchase by purchase. Your differentiation level will be all about the things you do to win the relationships and strengthen the bond between your brand and people over time.

This process will also reveal quite clearly which role your brand plays in its category. This is important, because, as we know, each role comes with a set of expectations. Is your brand the de facto market leader, but does not take responsibility for growing the category as it should? A challenger brand must address the issue of exactly what it does that challenges the market leader or the entire category. Is that challenge understood in the market? And do customers appreciate it? A pioneer must decide whether its pioneer job – such as establishing a sub category or transforming a category entirely – is done or if there is still new frontier to settle.

How are the criteria fulfilled?

Once the list of selection criteria relevant to your brand has been refined and reduced down to a manageable number, the real job begins. It's at this point in the process you define as clearly as possible exactly how your brand fulfils each of the criteria, and how, through doing so, it plays out its role in the category.

For example, all makers of cars must innovate, but we expect different things from different car brands. We expect Volvo to innovate in ways that make us even safer driving its cars, and we expect BMW to innovate to further enhance the driving experience.

When you have your chosen criteria listed and sorted, you have decided how your brand fulfils them, and you may also have formulated a descriptive headline for each of the rocket levels, the time has come to script everything in such a way as to turn it into an effective decision making tool. Make sure all the items are consistent, that they don't contradict each other, and all support and lead up to that which makes your brand unique right at the top of the rocket.

Rocket in action

Organisations that want to show all employees exactly how they are, in fact, brand builders in the way they go about their day-to-day business, whether their job is in product development, HR or customer support, will find the differentiation rocket a useful tool to serve this purpose. It's also a useful at-a-glance overview that helps management stay on top of which parts of the business have the greatest impact on the brand. When things happen in the competitive arena to suggest changes are afoot in your industry, the rocket is a great starting point for a thorough review of the current and future relevance of your brand's differentiated position.

Consider, for example, the banking industry. Not that long ago their IT strategies related primarily to the security of operations and cost management. Going forward, there is no doubt that digital solutions essentially carry the relationship between the bank and its customers, which in turn makes the digital solutions central to people's understanding of the bank's brand. So, it is apparent that this change in the importance of the bank's IT strategy not only impacts the business in a fundamental way, but also the brand. What kind of bond can we forge between a bank and its customers through digital interfaces? What are the right digital services for our brand of bank or financial institution? How will our decision to develop our own solutions, or develop in collaboration with others, or acquire/distribute the services of other brands impact our brand? How do we now position our brand in relation to issuers of credit cards, global digital platforms and popular gadgets, when it comes to ownership of, let's say, payment solutions? Who will people seek economic advice from in the future and how will they want to organise their finances? Obviously, a differentiation rocket can't answer these questions in and of itself, but it can be an effective tool in your effort to correlate your business and your brand.

When you feel that you're done creating your differentiation rocket, make sure you also calibrate the final version by checking it with representatives from your market, customers and organisation.

- Do employees recognise the key criteria?
- Do customers accept the stipulated reasons for selecting your brand?
- Is the difference between your brand and the competition clear enough?

Now, you are ready to mobilise your entire organisation and make sure everyone understands how their actions and decisions – large and small – strengthen your brand. (You'll learn more about how to do that in the integration section of this book.) First, show how your organisation fulfils the various criteria at the moment and how it's playing out its role in the category. Next, show people your brand's future position. Then show them how to fill the gap between the two, and empower them to do so. And that's how you find yourself with an organisation where everyone plays an active part in building your brand as the most natural part of doing his or her day-to-day job.

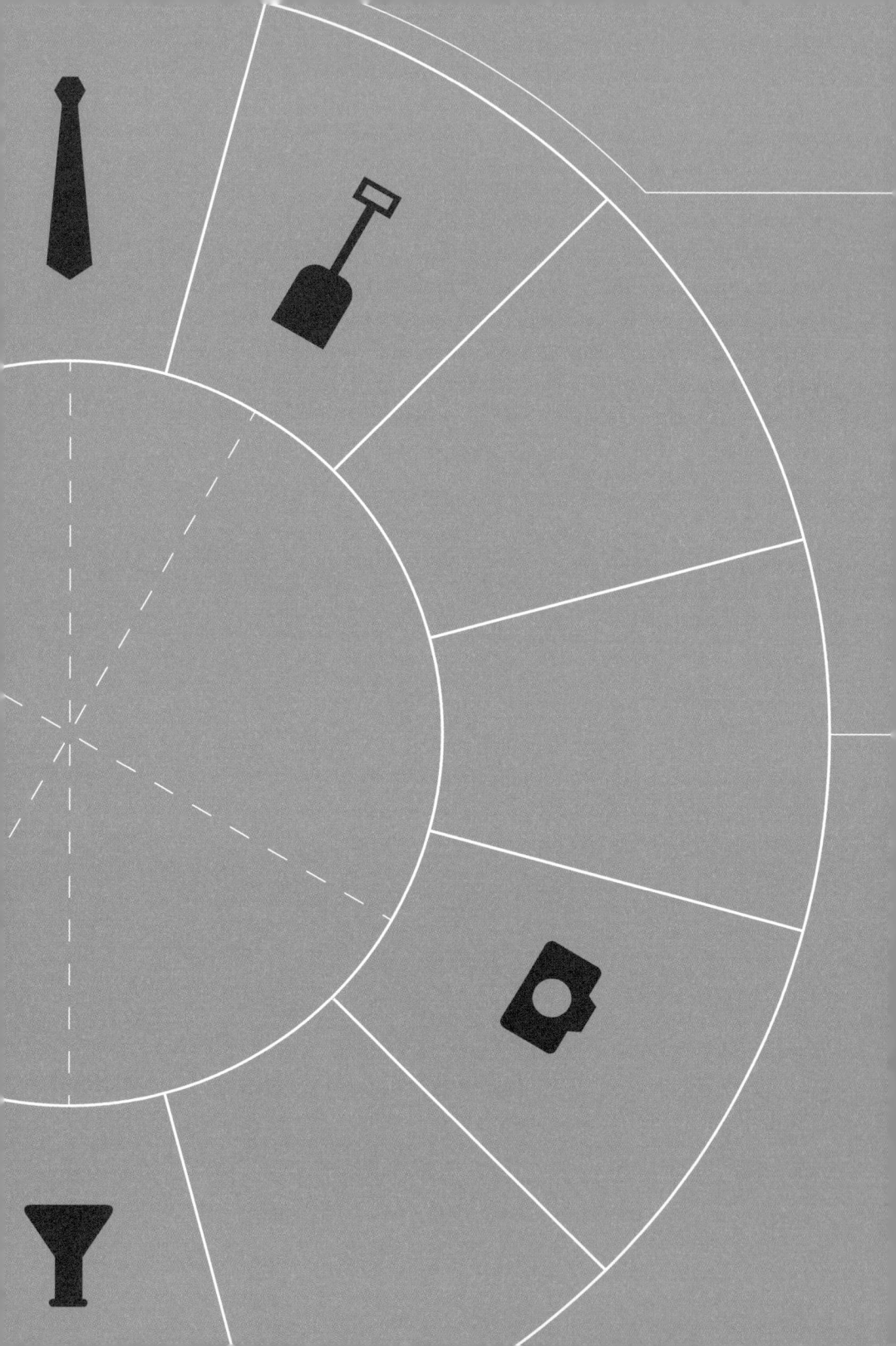

Identity

Archetypes

Identity prism

Branding, its origins and tasks

Imagine women gathering at the water well, for example in ancient Egypt, and the chatter turning to the relative merits of the different water pot makers. One makes pots that rarely break, but are a bit on the heavy side. Another makes pots that balance easily atop the head, but are a little fragile. Some of the women prefer one, some prefer the other.

Archaeologists have discovered trademarks on merchandise that's thousands of years old – from China, India and the Nile delta. The first marks of this kind identified its producer. Later guild marks became a kind of collective guarantee of quality that extended to all the guild's members. An artisan would want to produce wares of high quality, to secure income to the family and earn the respect of his or her peers. Even later the trademark would replace and become a stand-in for the personal relationship that existed between the potter, carpenter and cobbler and their customers.

As a result of the industrial revolution, the importance of trademarks increased even further. In a time of mass production people looked for something that could vouch for consistency of quality and act as a peg on which to hang the product's promises. The personal relationship with the producers of the products had become a thing of the past. Instead, seemingly identical products sought to establish – through the use of advertising and mass communication – associations between their brand and various attractive properties and characteristics. Thus began the development of brands as we know them today, animated into full blown brand personalities or identities that we relate to in an emotional way.

> **"** Today, we have much higher expectations from a brand than a simple guarantee that the product works. We can come to admire brands, swear eternal loyalty or be downright disgusted by them.

Many of the best known industrial brands go by the name of their founders, whether Ford, Edison General Electric (now GE), or Selfridges, and probably not for vanity reasons alone.

Today, we have much higher expectations from a brand than a simple guarantee that the product works. We can come to admire brands, swear eternal loyalty or be downright disgusted by them. To evoke this level of emotion and involvement, brands need personalities – that is, a brand identity.

The brand identity serves three obvious purposes. All three are important to establishing and strengthening the bond between the brand and the people that relate to it.

Firstly, people must be able to *identify* the brand.
As long as the brand is a product or a family of products, it's a relatively simple matter to signal identification on the product itself or its packaging. When it comes to services, however, identification can be more complicated. Whether we are

talking about digital or physical services, their spaces, people or service designs must have some sort of recognisable uniformity. Functionality, language or adherence to certain standards can also play a part in enforcing recognisability and hence identity.

Also, the brand must be *identical* over time and from touch point to touch point. What if a Coca-Cola tasted differently every time? Or, let's say, the clothing retailer H&M started charging Hermès prices? Brands make it easy for people to choose by being consistent. People want to know what to expect even when a brand crosses product or category boundaries.

Last, but certainly not least, people want to be able to *identify with* a brand. Not necessarily to the level of Harley-Davidson riders tattooing the logo onto their bodies, but we want to be able to comfortably stand by our choice to buy and use the brands we choose. The closer the relationship, the more loyal we tend to be, just like in our relationships to human beings. If people don't identify with your brand, buying or using it is a matter of indifference or worst case, utterly taboo. Indifference may be the greatest threat to brands right now. The selection of choices is almost endless, so unless you can create some sort of identification with your brand in the minds of its users, they'll happily select whatever is cheaper or more readily available next time around.

In this section of the book devoted to identity, we introduce two different tools to help you better understand some of the mechanisms behind establishing and maintaining that bond with customers and users. The first tool is the use of archetypes. Archetypes are used in the process of getting to the bottom of what really motivates people to bond with your brand. The second tool is Kapferer's identity prism (2012, p. 158). The prism functions as a kind of 360 degree model to help us define the brand identity through investigation of six central aspects of the brand itself, its target audience and the culture shared by the two.

In combination, using these two tools will help you provide a good description of both the *who* and the *how* of your brand identity.

Chapter 5
Archetypes

Imagine that you get to pick a car, any car, and drive it around, free of charge for the next three years. The following rules apply, you must choose right now, and no one can know that you're not paying for it.

Perhaps your first impulse is to choose a super fancy car. But your next thought might just be "can I show up to work in it" or "what will my neighbours think"? Perhaps you have some concerns about how much your selected car would reveal about what really motivates your choice? In the end, you'd be likely to end up selecting a brand and car model that you like and that you feel becomes you and your lifestyle.

Your thoughts during the above experiment may not have been primarily about the cars' functional characteristics, but rather considerations around what your choice of car says about you. Did it pop into your head that you'd like to be seen in a Porsche – or perhaps absolutely not? Did it make you feel boring when your first thought was Mercedes? Did you indulge in the dream of a Jaguar, but afraid that your friends and colleagues would think you a show off, decide to pass?

Archetypes help brands build relationships

In a world where the sheer amount of offers and choices is overwhelming, it's crucial for brands to really understand what it is that motivates people to select their products or services above those of the competition.

Your brand needs a personality to make people want to form a relationship of trust with or even grow to like it. It's easier for people to bond, and continue to develop that bond, with personalities they feel that they understand. And the beauty of the archetypes is that we all get them. Because the archetypes represent common human needs and motivations, we all recognise them intuitively. That's why we recognise and understand brand identities that are based on an archetypical identity. Now that we know how important it is for brands to develop this kind of relationship with their customers, and that a single brand promise no longer can be trusted to carry a loyal

> **Brands with a clear archetypical identity outperform brands that vacillate between two archetypes, and that even these outperform brands that are all over the place, archetypically speaking.**

relationship, it can be helpful to turn to the archetypes as a brand identity tool. It was well documented, for example in *The Hero and the Outlaw* by Mark and Pearson (2001) that brands with a clear archetypical identity outperform brands that vacillate between two archetypes, and that even these outperform brands that are all over the place, archetypically speaking.

Our work with and understanding of archetypes used for branding purposes comes mainly from what we learned from *The Hero and the Outlaw* (Mark & Pearson, 2001). However, the chapter was also inspired by *Archetypes in branding* by Hartwell and Chen (2012) and its exposition of 60 archetypes (5 variants of each of the most common 12).

Archetypes can be an inspiring and useful approach to:
- kicking off your brand identity work.
- understanding a competitive arena from an outsider's perspective – what is it about the various brands that's attractive to people?
- understanding the dynamics of your category. Is everyone the same, or are the different brands appealing to different customer motivations?
- understanding unwritten cultural rules and values.
- engaging the people in your organisation in your brand identity development in a way that most people enjoy. Very often, the link between their day-to-day job and the archetypical identity is immediate and intuitive, which makes it quite easy for people to see themselves as representatives of the brand.

You'll find descriptions of the main characteristics of each archetype, and a few examples of each, at the end of this chapter. Before going into detail about the individual archetypes however, you can read more about what archetypes are and how to use them.

An axis of human needs

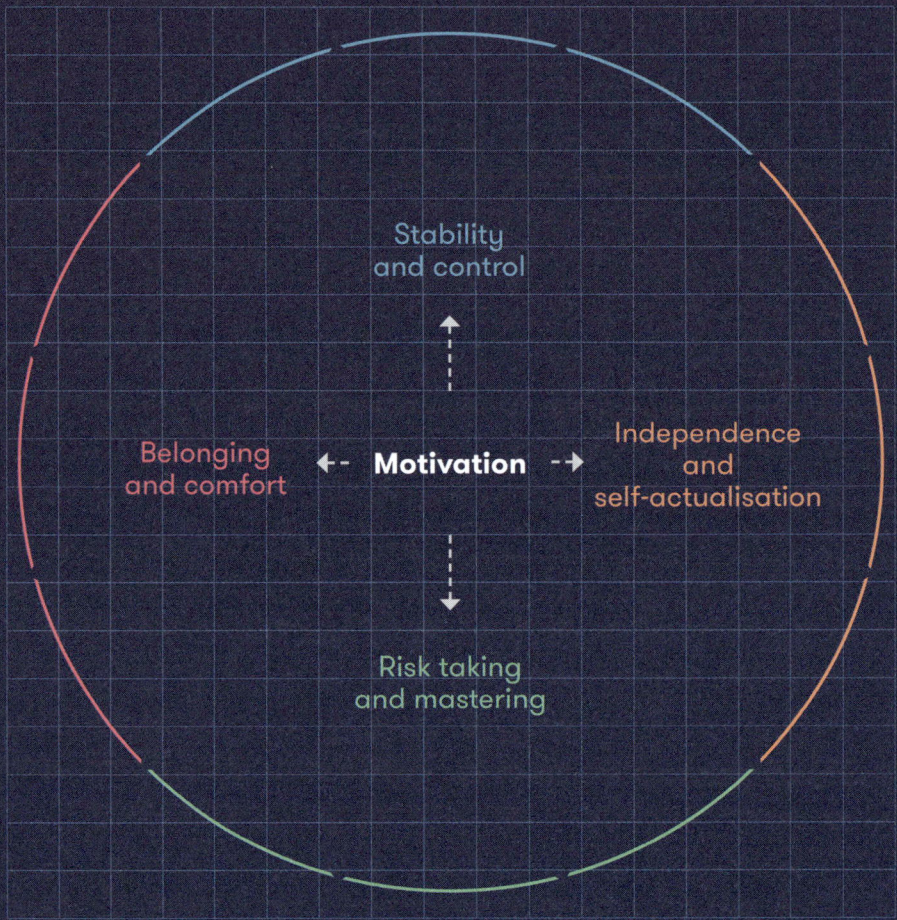

Understanding the axis

Our most fundamental needs are organised along two lines between at least partially opposing needs. The vertical line covers the span between our need for stability and control on the top and our need for risk taking and mastery at the bottom. The horizontal line goes from our needs for belonging and comfort on the one hand and independence and self-actualisation on the other.

What is an archetype?

An archetype is "a primordial image, character, or pattern of circumstances that recurs throughout literature and thought consistently enough to be considered a universal concept or situation" (Encyclopædia Britannica). We know the archetypes best from the writings of the psychologist Carl Jung, who formulated a theory of a "collective unconscious" where the archetypes, as representatives of varieties of human experience, have somehow been embedded and transferred from generation to generation.

For brand builders, archetypes provide a framework that helps us simplify and select the key characteristics of a brand's identity. Archetypes are representations of personality types, and as such they help us define the most important brand identity characteristics depending on the kind of relationship the brand is aiming to build or strengthen between itself and its customers.

As a framework, it's quite rich. The archetype axis takes into account the complexity of human motivations. This is helpful for brands that want to build great and dynamic brand personalities that stay far clear of clichés, but are nevertheless recognisable as a variant of an archetype. A cliché in this context could be a rebel brand that's cursing in every direction, in opposition to everyone. Such clichés are boring at best and seriously annoying at worst, which makes it a poor foundation for a brand indeed. Especially if your aim is a brand identity that people will care about and cheer for. The archetypical rebel should be seen as having a clear and strong set of values, even if the values may be at odds with those of the establishment. Consider how PayPal entered the scene, disruptive in nature, in opposition to old money, assuming the risk of peer to peer transactions so that we don't have to.

Whether we are talking about film, TV-series, books, plays, games, songs or art, the strongest characters are both archetypal and something else, something extra and unique. The same goes for brands. Before a bond can be forged between a brand and people, we need to get to know them. We need to understand the brand's general situation (category, role, differentiation as discussed in the Positioning part of this book), the relationship between the brand and its customers, and what the brand wants to do for each individual and for the world at large.

When Coca-Cola said *Open Happiness*, it said that Coke is a brand that wants to contribute to happy moments and be a part of the feeling that, fleeting or lasting, things are pretty good. Similarly, Prudential insurance – in name as well as its rock of Gibraltar logo – signals that it is a brand you can trust to take care of your assets.

Which personality type we gravitate towards depends entirely on what motivates us to seek a particular kind of product or service in the first place. What is the real need we are seeking to satisfy by the brand?

What archetypes represent

You may be familiar with Maslow and his hierarchy of human needs? You know, the one with physiological needs at the bottom, next comes safety needs, the need for love and belonging, followed by esteem needs for recognition by others and finally self actualisation needs at the top of the hierarchy? Ideally, we seek to fulfil all these needs, but if a need that belongs to a lower level in the hierarchy is unfulfilled (for example basic safety) the motivation to seek fulfilment of needs higher up in the hierarchy (for example recognition of our accomplishments) is low.

As you will notice when working with the archetypes, this is a slightly different way of organising human needs. To illustrate what each of the archetypes represent, they are distributed around an axis of simultaneous but opposing needs. The vertical line covers the span between our need for stability and control on the top and our need for risk taking and mastery at the bottom. This span is easy to recognise in children. Children love habits, a familiar stuffed animal and grown ups that can be trusted. However, there's also a whole world out there to explore and lots of new and wonderful things to try for the first time. When things inevitably go wrong or become frightening, it's a quick journey to the safety of a familiar lap.

In the grown up world we see similar tendencies, for example when the world seems somehow less secure and things less certain than they used to be. When times are good, people leave secure jobs to realise entrepreneurial or creative dreams, young people choose professions with notoriously low job security, but with great opportunities for creative expression. In harder times, on the other hand, nursing and teaching colleges may note surges in number of applications and people tend to hold on to the jobs they have.

When building a brand, it's useful to know where in this axis to place people's motivations. Is your brand a safe choice for people who are motivated by a need for a brand they can trust always (Tampax), or is your brand for people who couldn't care less about the conventional choices of others (Brewdog)?

The horizontal line goes from our needs for belonging and comfort on the one hand and independence and self-actualisation on the other. Again, the span between the two sides are easily recognised in ourselves. Humans are herd animals and need to belong and enjoy the company of other humans. At the same time, we also

Archetypes

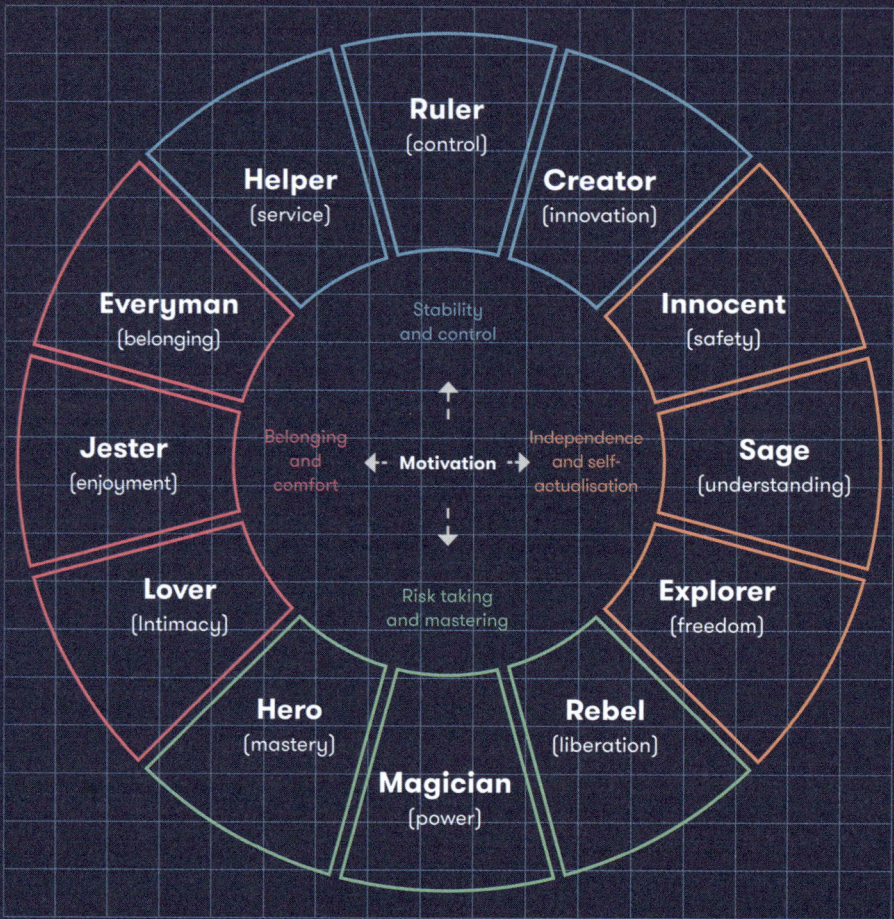

How to read the archetype wheel

The archetypes are representations of the various human motivations in their purest form. Use the archetype wheel to understand which personality traits are key to people's relationship with your brand.

You'll discover that the traits they value the highest will be connected to the need they are motivated to fulfil when gravitating towards your brand.

want to be seen as unique independent individuals as we seek to realise projects small and large throughout our lives. As a brand, Facebook represents an identity that takes responsibility for fulfilling our need for community and belonging. The New York Times appeals to our need for being a person that is knowledgeable and up to date.

The archetype wheel
The 12 archetypes most commonly used for branding purposes are distributed at the four extremities of the axis, three archetypes for each.

At the stability and control extremity we find the three archetypes that represent these needs in slightly different ways. The Helper is caring, the Ruler has authority and the Creator represents enduring structures. At the opposite end of the line you find the archetypes that represent change and risk taking. The Hero fights his battles for the sake of others, the Magician has strong (perhaps also hidden) powers for change, and the Rebel goes her own way in opposition to the powers that be.

On the left hand side of the horizontal line we find the three archetypes that represent belonging and comfort. The Jester is an agent of fun, the Everyman represents consensus and community, and the Lover stands for sensuality and intimacy between people.

At the final extremity, we find the archetypes that represent our needs for independence and self-actualisation. The Innocent represents wonder and new ideas, the Sage represents truth rather than consensus and the Explorer will tread new paths in his search for the perfect and authentic.

In practice, we seek out helper brands when we feel in need of protection from harm. In the car category, Volvo is the clearest

helper brand. Volvo promises us that it provides the safest cars to appeal to our motivation to have someone (Volvo) take responsibility for our safety.

While working with archetypes can help brands craft identities that really stand out, it's nevertheless common for the different brands in a category to have nearly identical brand identities. Appealing to exactly the same customer motivation as everyone else is a missed opportunity for differentiation by distinct personality. Look at the insurance industry. Helper brand after helper brand, which seems a pity considering that standing out from the competition in your category is a huge component of brand building.

To make it just a little more tricky – but also more useful

Let's take a look at the American underwear brand Victoria's Secret, taking into consideration what you already know about archetypes. Victoria's Secret is a brand that communicates through some of the most stunning women in the world wearing next to nothing. Surely, Victoria's Secret is acting out the archetypical identity of a lover brand?

Hang on a minute. Could it be argued that rather than Victoria's Secret being a lover brand, it's the entire women's underwear category that evokes the lover archetype? (The athletic underwear and safe-to-boil categories probably excepted). With this in mind, it's more interesting to look at the Victoria's Secret brand compared to other ladies' underwear brands – Victoria's Secret models having fun on the catwalk, over the top costumes, performers joining them on stage, all televised as prime time entertainment. Girls just wanna have fun it seems – granted we're talking about the most

> " Your brand identity described as a version of an archetype will, in other words, have at least two layers: the archetype of your category and your brand's archetype when everything that's associated with the category and not your brand, has been peeled away.

desirable girls on the planet, but nevertheless they seem such a happy bunch – which makes Victoria's Secret a jester brand in all its festive glory.

<u>Your brand identity described as a version of an archetype will, in other words, have at least two layers: the archetype of your category and your brand's archetype when everything that's associated with the category and not your brand, has been peeled away.</u>

If you're not that into ladies' underwear, let's illustrate the same principle by looking at the auto industry. As a category, cars are explorers. Almost every car commercial shows cars speeding through exotic landscapes in some shape or form. Cars are about going places you otherwise might not reach. And yet, the only car brands to fully embrace the explorer archetype fully are brands like Land Rover and Jeep. And these are not exactly the biggest brands in cars. When I ask people, in workshops or during presentations, they usually agree that Mercedes is a ruler brand, Volvo is a helper, Toyota is an everyman and

Jaguar a lover brand, to name but a few. So, we all buy cars to get from A to B, but we each want to get there in different style. Some of us like to ride safely, some unnoticeably and some with swagger and so on all the way around the archetype or identity wheel.

And just one more thing …

In certain cases a third archetype consideration will be necessary, and that's when your brand is taking on an active role in driving a change that affects people or catches their attention in a very specific way. As a brand, Tesla is acting out the Apple playbook from Steve Jobs' magician brand era. However, Tesla is also taking on the role of climate pioneer and has, at least to some extent, assumed the explorer identity as it dares us to leave our fossil fuel dependency behind and explore the limits of battery technology and overall car performance.

This may seem like a complicating factor, but in practice it usually isn't. In fact, the ability to sort category traits, from identity traits as well as characteristics of a particular task at hand, is liberating. There will usually be traits that people expect from all players in a category, your brand included. However, it's much more interesting to discover which traits motivate people to seek out your brand above other brands in the category. These are the characteristics

> The ability to sort category traits, from identity traits as well as characteristics of a particular task at hand, is liberating.

that carry people's emotional bond with your brand and should therefore form the foundation of your brand identity. A brand's archetype also determines what kind of stories we tell about it, and this is due in part to its role in the competitive arena and in part the role we allow it to play in our lives.

If we take a look at the low cost airline Ryanair, we see an everyman brand (air travel everybody can afford) that picked a fight with market leading ruler brand British Airways over what could be considered a reasonable price to pay to fly from Dublin to London or the other way around. When Ryanair received its license to fly this route, it cut the price in half and then some. As a result, the incumbents had to slash their prices and thus started the first fare war in Europe. Others were to follow. Ryanair has outgrown its license to act the part of David against Goliath, but is still very much an everyman carrier and keeps the price point pressure up so that we can all take cheap holidays together.

Making use of archetypes in your brand building

The archetypes help us understand both what motivates people to approach a category, and the individual brands in it. Obviously, how clearly we associate a category or a brand with an archetype varies. We buy insurance primarily to feel more safe and because it's the responsible thing to do. An insurance provider that does not provide this sense of security is unthinkable. Whether it is for this reason alone all insurance brands are so similar, I could not say for sure, but it is uncanny how they all use symbols (steady rock, lifebuoy) and language (Assurance, Prudence, Fidelity) to evoke the helper archetype – secure, caring, polite, looking out for us and that which we hold dear.

The car category on the other hand illustrates well how different brands evoke different archetypes with remarkable clarity. Most people respond intuitively to the different brand identities, responding consciously and subconsciously to the motivations/needs they represent. As mentioned, the explorer is omnipresent in car advertising – shiny cars on winding roads along beaches and over mountains before they come to rest at the fancy hotel or safely back home where we belong. But who's driving? How many in the car? What's in the boot? What are they doing and where are they going? These are things that change depending on the archetype of the car brand identity. Thus, which car make and brand people choose is much more of a personal statement about our own identity than where you buy your insurance is.

A strong brand identity is one that recognises the archetype of its category and understands how to be both useful to and enjoyable for its customers through the way their products or services play a role in people's lives. If, in addition, the brand's organisation understands the archetypal identity of its brand, it's much easier to consistently make choices small or large that strengthen the brand identity. It is easier for this kind of organisation to find the confidence to watch other brands do things differently, in line with their roles and identities, without a sense of panic to catch up. That's how they do it and that's fine. Our way is this way. All vacuum cleaners must be able to suck up dust and debris, but a rugged fellow might prefer to do his cleaning using a Dyson – a creator brand representing performance, technology and innovation – rather than a hot pink Senz, which seems to channel a kind of glamorous lover archetype.

First category, then brand, and finally role

The quickest route to the best and most fit for purpose brand identity is to start wide and work your way in. Start by your category's archetype, then look for archetypical identity traits in your competitors' brand identities and your own. Finally, ask yourself whether there is a particular role in the competitive arena your brand has to take on right now, and whether the role has archetypical qualities in and of itself.

There are, at least, two approaches to this task of narrowing in on the right archetype.

One way is to take your brand positioning as a starting point.
Is your category unclear to people (hot dogs made from fish), is the competition undifferentiated and characterised by generic providers (hotel booking) or are people faced with a wide range of incomprehensible substitutes (fast food)? Is there a clear split between people's expectations to the alternatives in the category in general and expectations to your brand in particular? Virgin Atlantic's Steve Ridgway talked about his surprise at the overwhelmingly positive response to its 20-year anniversary video Still Red Hot (McKinsey Quarterly April 2011). It made the company really appreciate that it is the brand's way of being different to everyone else in the airline industry that attracts people. As a brand, Virgin Atlantic doesn't compete on the same criteria as the rest, but rather on its ability to keep surprising people and *fly in the face of ordinary*.

The other approach is to start by understanding people's motivations for buying the products or services of your category.
T-Mobile is a challenger brand that took upon itself to liberate people from the lock-in strategies of its competitors, as a kind

of hero brand or at least taking a heroic role in this respect. It learned that people were actually getting really frustrated by lock-in strategies as well as their current providers' impossible-to-understand price plans. T-Mobile used that knowledge about people's motivations to craft a new kind of entirely voluntary and transparent relationship (Prophet 2017). Because the company is well aware that customers will remain as long as they are happy, but that they're under no obligation to stay if not, the brand is constantly finding new ways to please.

> **❝ It's exciting to notice how people, as soon as they become familiar with them, easily identify brands, competitors and even sometimes themselves as archetypes.**

Off to a good start

Working with archetypes, it's exciting to notice how people, as soon as they become familiar with them, easily identify brands, competitors and even sometimes themselves as archetypes.

The archetype alone, however, will not deliver a winning brand personality. When you have defined your chosen brand archetype, deciding what your version of that archetype is going to be and refining your brand identity into a winning personality is still a sizeable job. As we know, great story telling requires interesting, many-faceted characters.

What is it that makes your brand credible? How exactly does a brand realise its helper identity, or rebel or explorer identities? For each archetype there is room for a wide range of different characters. And this is where the identity prism developed by Jean-Noël Kapferer (2012) comes in handy. The prism helps brand builders analyse and define brand identities in much greater detail. You will learn about the identity prism in the next chapter of this book, but first a short introduction to the 12 most important archetypes.

A short introduction to the 12 archetypes

In the following you'll get to know the most important archetypes, and hopefully find some insight to inspire your brand identity work. There's a lot more to learn about using archetypes for brand identity purposes, and you can read all about it in *The Hero and the Outlaw* (Mark and Pearson 2001), but this is a pretty good start.

Identity - Archetypes

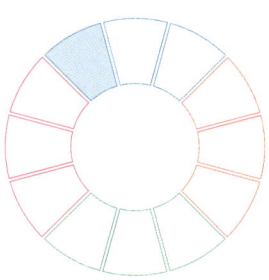

The Helper

The Helper

The helper's motivation is to protect people from harm. People seek out helper brands when they need to feel secure and protected, or to demonstrate how they themselves are the kind of people that care about the safety and well being of others.

You'd struggle to find a clearer example of a helper than the Save the Children brand. Another one is Toms who helps children get an education by donating a pair of shoes to children that need them to walk to school, for every pair of shoes sold. Naturally, this charitable aspect of the shopping experience may also be helpful in alleviating retail guilt in Toms shoes shoppers. If you ask people to assign archetypes to countries, they tend to name Sweden the helper – perhaps due to strong brands like Volvo and IKEA. Volvo is a helper brand through and through, and it's fairly easy to cast IKEA with its vision "to create a better everyday life for the many people" in the helper role.

Market leaders – and monopolists in particular – have a tendency to assume helper identities to offset any misgivings we might have about their powerful market position or notions that the brands may be abusing that power. One example of a market leader that has successfully taken on the helper role is the National Health

Service in the UK and its well known and much respected NHS brand. Where it could potentially have struggled under the sheer size and complexity of its operations, it's managed to become a symbol of universal access to quality care and is one of the top 25 brands in Britain (Prophet 2017).

If you'd like to watch a helper brand play out this role with no holds barred, please enjoy the Procter & Gamble (P&G) ad launched for the London 2012 Olympics. The ad named "Best job" is a tribute to mothers. With its "thank you mom" tag line the ad celebrates the importance of mothers' behind-the-scenes efforts to the athletes' achievements – and also celebrates the mothers' joy in their children's success.

Helpers can also be known as mother, father, big sister/brother, nurse, guide, saint, altruist, mentor, coach, angel, fairy godmother, good Samaritan, healer.

Identity - Archetypes

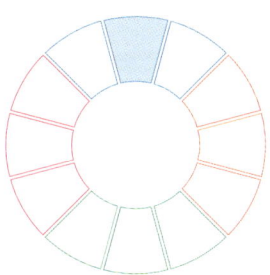

The Ruler

The Ruler

The ruler is driven by a sense of responsibility and will exercise leadership to ensure the best possible conditions for organisations, societies or families to thrive. With this leadership comers power, status and prestige. Ruler brands must strike this balance between responsibility and privilege. Market leaders, for example, will often take responsibility for growing its entire category. Mercedes with its promise of *Das beste oder nichts* is a good ruler brand representative. Ruler brands will often be the first choice for people looking to demonstrate success.

In low involvement categories such as banking or telecom, or products and services that are infrastructure-like in general, people often choose ruler brands that represent stability and control.

Uber can be seen as a contemporary ruler brand. The name itself is a clue, and as is the first tag line Everyone's private driver – such as a ruler might have – and recently Uber has taken upon itself to carry the standard for the sharing economy. When Uber sets up operations in a new city it feels more like a conquest than a regular expansion. However, Uber seems to be shifting its brand identity towards a more community oriented everyman. The visual identity is no longer black and blue, but includes softer shades like white and green. The web site shows friendly ordinary-looking people, the new slogan seems to be simply Get there, and on the Uber Wikipedia entry you'll find the rather sweet explanation that Uber is a German slang word for super. We'll see.

A country that evokes the ruler brand identity even in its name is Great Britain. Tony Blair attempted a repositioning of the country brand with the Cool Britannia concept. Today the ruler is back and the national brand building efforts have embraced the word Great in a meaningful way.

Rulers can also be known as king, leader, father, steady rock, pater familias, master, role model, politician, boss, judge, lawmaker.

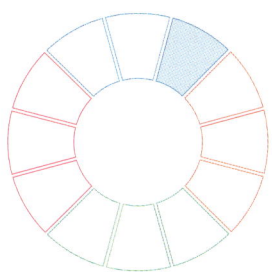

The Creator

The Creator

The creator represents creativity and innovation. Ideas start out as a stirring, a thought or a slight unease and a wish to make something better, more beautiful, faster or different altogether. The creator gives these ideas concrete form or provides lasting structures for their realisation.

LEGO may just be the ultimate creator brand. Our motivation for buying LEGO products is not primarily about the creative genius of LEGO, although LEGO is undoubtedly a hugely creative organisation. Instead we are motivated by a wish to provide opportunities for our children to find creative expression and develop their creativity.

Similarly, Adobe creates products that enable creative people in their expression, collaboration and production of creative deliverables. The Snøhetta architects and designers create physical expressions through which cities and countries find expression of their identities, and Mini lets you customise your car in a way that makes the car an extension of yourself.

It appears Apple is now looking to build its brand identity as a version of this archetype. If you take a closer look at recent Apple communication you'll find a new emphasis on all the things you can do as long as you have the latest "i" or Apple gadget. Just like the Apple Watch promised that it knows you better so it can push you further (Apple 2018).

YouTube is a young creator brand, providing infrastructure for people to create, find and share video content; a platform that has given many people the opportunity to seek fame, status and, for a lucky few, even significant financial success.

Creators can also be known as inventor, inspirer, innovator, renewer, artist, entrepreneur, auteur.

Identity - Archetypes

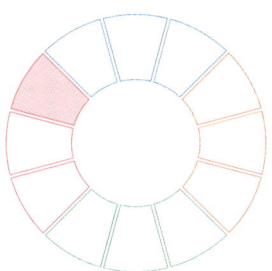

The Everyman

The Everyman

The everyman archetype is more than anything about belonging. Humans are herd animals, and even if we want to feel special, it's nice to know that there are other people like us. The everyman is someone who is always there in our everyday lives, stands for solid and genuine values that can be trusted. Several beer brands evoke this archetype. Beer is also connected somehow to football, the everyman's archetypical sport.

Holiday Inn with its *Pleasing people the world over* is a clear everyman brand in the mid price hotel category, which most people will recognise as such. Citizen M has chosen a fresh approach to boutique accommodation, which has traditionally belonged to the luxurious, unique and sophisticated. This hospitality brand claims to offer affordable boutique accommodation for a new kind of traveller, the type who crosses continents as naturally as other people cross streets – the mobile citizens of the world. While these people want affordable accommodation in a good location, and a certain level of comfort, they accept that rooms are small and make use of communal areas like the hotels' bars and libraries to relax, work or meet like-minded people. This kind of boutique is for all the new travellers.

Everyman can also be a good choice for challengers, particularly in categories dominated by very earnest, stuffy or sanctimonious brands. Samsung opposes Apple's our way or no way-attitude by providing a wide range of smartphones to suit every wallet and to serve every purpose. The same goes for Jack Daniels, the Tennessee Whiskey (technically bourbon) that started out as moonshine. In cosmetics, the Boots brand No. 7 is the cosmoceutical that doesn't promise the world, but actually delivers. Like a good everyman brand, it represents solid values and is simple, functional and affordable.

Despite its ivy league Harvard origins, the Facebook brand personifies the everyman archetype. Not only does Mark Zuckerberg look like the regular guy next door, but Facebook itself is a community. People sign up for Facebook to strengthen that sense of community with their 500 closest friends, and anyone else in the world with whom they want to connect. No wonder we react with outrage when we see Facebook exercising power too overtly – such as in the case of Facebook's censoring Nick Ut's famous photograph of a young Vietnamese girl fleeing a napalm attack. However, just like a good neighbour would, Facebook yielded to public opinion and decided to allow the photograph after all.

The everyman can also be known as salt of the Earth, worker, the good neighbour, citizen, ombudsman, spokesperson, regular Joe.

Identity - Archetypes

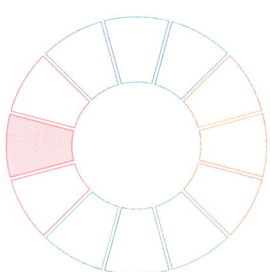

The Jester

The Jester

The jester is all about having fun – ideally together with other people. Jesters want everybody to have a good time and do not take themselves too seriously. A jester brand can be a breath of fresh air, particularly in categories characterized by proper, grown-up, high-status brands.

With its hippie identity Ben & Jerry's is a jester brand that has introduced a whole new set of selection criteria to the ice cream category. This brand has found room for premium as well as organic, a new visual as well as verbal language and sprinkled a solid helping of political activism on top. This a far cry from the dominant tropes of the category such as the sensuous stirring of cream into ice cream and bouncing berries in slow motion.

Two of my favourite jester brands are The New Yorker and The Economist. I'll not insist that they are jesters through and through, but both brands stand out with refreshingly tongue-in-cheek observations on the world of business and its leaders. The Economist's witty and intellectually arrogant ads may just be one of the most consistent communication concepts known to man.

The jester may be a good brand identity choice if your competitor is an everyman brand. It's hard to position a brand in opposition to a folksy, popular brand, but there's usually room for a player looking to have a little more fun and making an effort to bring some more life to the party. And once you've come to love a jester, the relationship tends to last.

The email marketing tool MailChimp, with its cheeky monkey that gives you a high five when you press the send button for your campaigns to go to (sometimes very long) lists of recipients, really takes the angst out of email marketing. The tool has all the bells and whistles, heavy analytics and automation options, but manages to be fun, irreverent and charming at the same time.

The jester brand identity is also an option if you're competing with a lover. As demonstrated by Victoria's Secret, being tall, dark and handsome is one thing, but making people laugh is pretty sexy too.

Jesters can also be known as joker, clown, life of the party, entertainer, fool, buffoon, prankster.

Identity - Archetypes

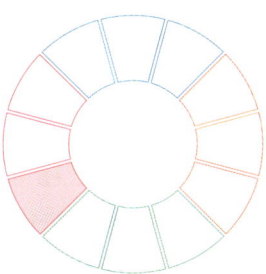

The Lover

The Lover

Italy is passion, France is romance, and both represent sensuality, intimacy and close relationships between people. As do roses, champagne and chocolate, which makes these gifts heavy with symbolic yearning for closeness.

It's almost touching to see otherwise sensible grown up men tenderly place the Jaguar logo in the lover's place in the archetype wheel when asked to distribute various car brands according to archetype. Whether they actually drive cars large or small, old or new, affordable or expensive, a line is drawn between rational thought and emotion. And there, beyond sense or reason, is the Jaguar.

We need lover brands in our lives, most of all in our everyday lives when we are also looking for pleasure and intimacy, albeit perhaps in smaller doses. Perhaps some Hershey kisses, a drop of Chanel no. 5 or a tumbler of Chivas Regal?

The lover archetype is not necessarily or overtly sexual, but represents closeness and intimacy. Tiffany is a brand that really understands the range and potential of the lover brand identity. Apparently, there is a "rule" in US culture (Financial Samurai 2016) that an engagement ring should be worth the equivalent of about two months' salary. This is of course contested – and silly if I may say so – but there can be little doubt that the ultimate engagement ring, regardless of size or price, comes in a Tiffany blue box. The pale blue box brings tidings of extraordinary love and affection. However, Tiffany recognises that love is more than romantic love and true to its archetypical identity provides gifts appropriate to any occasion where people may want to signal to each other "we belong together and I will be there for you always". As I write this, it's graduation time and Tiffany's web site displays beautiful jewellery parents might want to give their children to mark such an occasion.

Lovers can also be known as hedonist, boyfriend/girlfriend, partner, romantic, charmer, matchmaker.

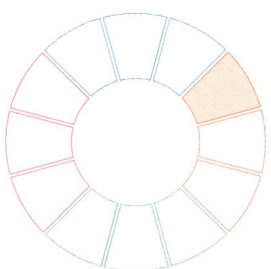

The Innocent

The Innocent

The innocent archetype represents the pursuit of happiness, peace and tranquility. The British juice and smoothie company so aptly named Innocent, is as clear an embodiment of this archetype as you're likely to find. The personality permeates everything from the ethically sourced fruit and vegetables that go into its beverages, to the compliment generator on its web site, which is tallying the number of compliments sent because "compliments are good" (Innocent 2017), never mind what it's got to do with making or selling juice.

Coca-Cola, McDonald's and Google are all brands that channel this archetype, which some people find hard to reconcile with the fact that each of these are savvy global giants. However, it's not as multinational corporate organisations they seek to personify the innocent, it's the brands that take on this archetypical identity. Coca-Cola's identity is closely linked to the optimism of 1960s suburbia. McDonald's gave families an excuse to eat out on a weeknight by recreating the happy family dinner table setting in its restaurants. The yellow M signalling a McDonald's is near is referred to as the golden arches and when you throw Ronald McDonald and play areas for children into the mix, the image is pretty clear.

We are familiar with the Google value *Don't be evil* and the "*I'm feeling lucky*" search button. Google's ambition to index all the information in the world and make it available to everybody is in line with both the naiveté and ambition of an innocent. With its *one less stranger* campaign, Airbnb tells us that people out there are simply friends you haven't met yet, and that inviting people to stay in your home or choosing to say in the homes of strangers is harmless and fun.

VW is also considered an innocent brand. VW is *Das Auto*, cars as they should be, no more no less. Whether the brand identity augmented our shock and consternation when VW was the first of the auto manufacturers to get caught cheating on its diesel emission levels, is a fair question to ask.

As a country brand, many people view Norway as an innocent – spectacular and seemingly untouched nature, midnight sun, northern lights, a royal family (like in the fairy tales), the Nobel peace prize and an egalitarian, well-organised society. Whether this is a country brand identity that does Norway any favours in terms of the international competition for talent, investment and tourism, I'll not be the judge.

The innocent can also be known as optimist, idealist, romantic, dreamer, seer, traditionalist, naturalist.

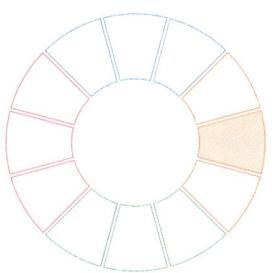

The Sage

The Sage

The sage seeks knowledge about the world and all things in it. Thus, the sage tends to appeal to other inquisitive characters; you know the kind of people who need to know why the sky is blue, how a combustion engine really works and how exactly to prepare the perfect steak.

Gallup promises to put leaders and organisations in a position to solve their most pressing problems by providing *Analytics & Advice About Everything That Matters.* The old broadsheet brands tend to have sage identities. The New York Times perhaps being their ultimate representative with its *All the News That's Fit to Print*, unchanged since 1897. The Guardian promises no less than *The Whole Picture.*

In this sense, the car brand Audi and sport nutrition brand Science in Sport, perhaps better known as SiS, could be considered close relatives. Audi says *Vorsprung durch Technik* and for SiS the name itself is an archetype giveaway. Audi will tell you exactly how its new led-lights adapt to the traffic, road and light conditions, and SiS will explain how its application of scientific method to its product development helps athletes perform. Here's an excerpt from a long description of the REGO Rapid Recovery Plus "which has a complete amino acid profile to which we have added an additional 2g of Leucine and 5g of L-Glutamine to support muscle protein synthesis" (SiS 2017). Combined with its claim that 34 medals in the 2016 Rio Olympics were "Science in Sport fuelled" we understand that this sage knows what its talking about.

The sage archetype also represents a wish to spread knowledge, to the benefit and enjoyment of others, much like a David Attenborough-like character. Harvard and McKinsey are strong on research, consulting and education, both in terms of academic research and popularising that research through publications in Harvard Business Review and McKinsey Quarterly. Thus, these brands encompass the search for knowledge through academic research and the role as educator of business leaders. The motivation for both tasks is rooted in an ambition to make things better through the application of knowledge.

The kitchen has recently become an important arena for sage brands. Whether your new obsession is molecular gastronomy, sous-vide or something else, there's no end to the specialized equipment required. One might also wonder if the objective of these new amateur chefs is a truly wonderful meal, or whether mastering the new techniques and equipment in and of themselves is the true objective.

Sages can also be known as expert, teacher, mentor, detective, interpreter, philosopher, oracle, academic, scientist, thinker, advisor, nerd.

Identity - Archetypes

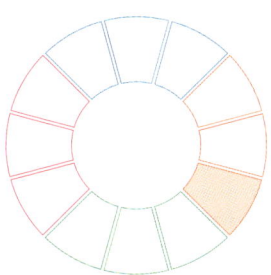

The Explorer

The Explorer

The explorer is independent, brave and adventurous. Explorers seek enlightenment by traveling to new places, trying new things and pushing their own boundaries. They look for authenticity, an experience of true liberty and free expression.

The best known explorer brand is probably Starbucks with its siren logo, named as it is after the first mate on the whaling ship in the novel *Moby Dick* (Herman Melville 1851). Next time you visit a Starbucks, take a look around and you may discover ship and seafaring artefacts and other objects that suggest exotic locations. In addition to the physical signs of its explorer brand identity, Starbucks also introduced Americans to coffee from named, faraway, coffee producing locations. Whereas coffee used to be a generic product, Starbucks taught us how to custom order unique and elaborate coffee based beverages exactly to our own taste. In fact, Starbucks made us queue around the block to pay for coffee that we'd otherwise get for free in the office.

Any category that has an element of exploration, might want to consider this archetype for its brand identity. NASA is a clear explorer brand that appeals not only to researchers and astronauts, but everyone who might find themselves contemplating the endless expanse of the universe on a starry night from time to time. The explorer archetype is also the brand identity of choice for many an outdoors apparel brand such as The North Face, Patagonia and Napapijri. The latter is Italian in origin, but the name is a Finnish word for the arctic circle (almost), it's owned by Americans, headquartered in Switzerland and last, but not least, sports the Norwegian flag in its logo.

Just like the sage, the explorer can be a good archetype choice for brands not positioned for the mass market, but rather targets smaller, often more demanding, customer segments. In professional services in particular, there will always be some that are known for being ahead of their industry and these may be preferred by innovators looking to push ahead into the future. These are professional service brands that tend to be chosen by customers that have strategic reasons of their own for wanting to be early movers. These customers will recognise and appreciate the risk of operating in unchartered territory, will be willing to pay more for highly bespoke services, exclusivity and an opportunity to influence the direction of its industry.

Explorers can also be known as adventurer, traveller, researcher, pioneer, nomad, pilgrim, individualist, seeker.

Identity - Archetypes

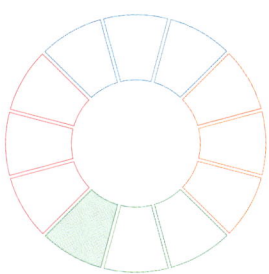

The Hero

The Hero

The courageous hero is willing to take risks, to take on challenges and achieve victories – more than anyone else and usually on behalf of someone else. The hero appeals to people looking to be the best they can be, and inspires people to develop their talents and strengths beyond what the regular guy will think possible.

Nike – named after a Greek goddess of victory – may be the ultimate hero brand, and also illustrates well how even an archetypical brand identity can develop over time. To begin with, the Nike brand was built through sponsorships and as supplier to the greatest athletes of the time, such as John McEnroe, Michael Jordan, Tiger Woods and Lance Armstrong. They were winners and Nike was the brand for winners. When the hero matures, however, the motivation shifts. Victory is no longer the goal in and of itself, but rather something that is sought on behalf of a community. The hero then applies his or her strengths and power for the sake of doing good in the world. In 2012, Nike launched the *Find your greatness* ad (Nike 2016) showing an overweight boy breathing heavily as he runs steadily towards us while a narrator builds up to the slogan attributed to Nike founder Bill Bowerman: *If you have a body, you're an athlete.*

The hero archetype may work well for your brand identity if you're championing an innovation or idea that could change the world, or if your product or service helps people perform to the very best and ideally beyond their abilities. The hero is also a good alternative archetype to the helper if your objective is tackling some sort of social issue and motivating people to show up and contribute is a part of it. The hero archetype can also be useful where risk is involved, such as when DHL promises that its express courier service will get your package to its destination in time no matter what.

Heros can also be known as warrior, crusader, saviour, soldier, combatant, team player, contestant, liberator.

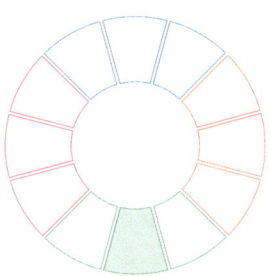

The Magician

The Magician

The magician's promise is that the impossible is possible and dreams do come true. In general, the magician is an archetype that works well for brands looking to bring something new into its category, transform it somehow or add a new layer of meaning.

Absolut vodka is a magician with transformative powers. You can tell by the bottle that evokes the medicinal flasks of ancient apothecaries. The brand's collaboration with Andy Warhol, another mystical and mythical character, is another hint. The brand has also launched new flavours based on herbs with mythical properties and entered into a series of projects with pioneers of art and culture that help Absolut continuously strengthen its magician attributes. (Absolut 2016)

I like to think of the restaurant Maaemo as a magician, both in terms of the restaurant experience itself, but also how this creative hothouse has transformed the way we think about gourmet food in general and the Norwegian food scene in particular. The name Maaemo, old Norse for mother earth (Maaemo 2016), signals that primal forces are at work. The way they experiment with local produce, traditional cooking and innovative gastronomy is alchemy-like. The result is a culinary experience so exceptional that according to the three stars awarded by the Michelin guide it's "worth a special journey".

Or how about CERN? The European Organization for Nuclear Research, where physicists and engineers are probing the fundamental structure of the universe using "the world's largest and most complex scientific instruments to study the basic constituents of matter – the fundamental particles" (Cern 2017) to advance our knowledge of the fundamental laws of nature, is surely a magician brand.

The magician may also appear in more mundane circumstances. Axe, for example, had no qualms suggesting that their deodorants, shampoos or body wash magically made men irresistible to women. In 2017 however, Axe moved with the times, now calling upon men to "Find your magic" and decide for themselves what it means to be a man (Unilever 2017). For most of us a little magic in our daily lives goes a long way, but sometimes that little spark of euphoria during a daily routine may be just what it takes to add a bit of colour and meaning to our lives.

Magicians can also be known as catalyst, visionary, charismatic, medicine man, scientist, inventor, alchemist.

Identity - Archetypes

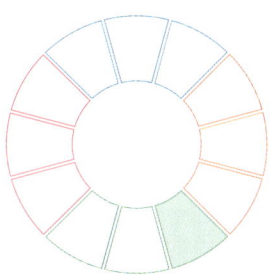

The Rebel

The Rebel

The rebel is a catalyst of profound change. The rebel challenges the establishment. The rebel can be recognised by his pent up energy and is often a freedom seeking outsider or dissenter.

The rebel opposes or is in conflict with the powers that be, the rulers and the establishment, in different ways. What it is about the establishment they find unacceptable will vary. However, if the rebel is to fit in, it is everyone else and not the rebel that needs to adapt. People fear as well as admire the rebel and the exciting, liberating, revolutionary energy they bring to the table for better and for worse.

You will nearly always find a rebel brand in categories where change is a constant. In art (Warhol, Hirst, Melgaard), music (Rolling Stones, Clash, Nirvana, Run D.M.C.) and fashion (Vivienne Westwood, Gaultier, Alexander McQueen) we need rebels to challenge the status quo and move the world forward.

The same applies to lifestyle categories where someone needs to step up and be the brand for people who like to think of themselves as different or not fitting in. Here's the Diesel manifesto: *We decode the world around us, take it apart and unlock what we thought we knew. We see differently and unite with those who see it too* (Diesel 2016). And there's Bed Head hair products: *Stand out, don't fit in!* (Bed Head 2016).

In crowded categories there'll usually be room for a rebel. As soon as a category becomes large enough, a rebel brand will pop up as if a matter of natural law.

Scottish brand BrewDog was set up in frustration by its founders who were sick and tired of industrial beers. While the brand has grown in size and reputation to become the global challenger to the established beer brands, it has maintained its contrary identity. In 2016 BrewDog was the fastest growing alternative beer in the UK and its Punk IPA the top IPA in terms of sales throughout Scandinavia (BrewDog 2016).

Rebels can also be known as activist, revolutionary, gambler, outlaw, outsider, wildcard, rabble-rouser.

Chapter 6
The identity prism

Before looking more closely at Kapferer's identity prism, it's worth revisiting the origins of brand identity, with which I introduced this section of the book. How and why did brand identity as we know it evolve? The most pervasive theories about the origin of branding take early craftspeople and the marks they placed on their products as a kind of signature as their starting point. "I made this," says the mark and "I guarantee the quality of this product and if you'd like something of equal quality next time around, look for my mark". This is also the logic that underpins modern trademarks. Whatever the organisation behind a brand promises, the mark guarantees. With industrialisation and mass production we started to endow trademarks with the added dimension of brand identity. Where individual craftsmen were replaced by impersonal factories, the individual relationship was transferred to the brand identity and our relationship with the brand identity became a substitute for the personal connection between producer and consumer on many levels. You may remember a distinction made at the beginning of this section between the three different jobs a brand does? Those three brand jobs are what we'll be exploring in this chapter of the book:

- The most basic job is to make sure people are able to *identify* the brand. They must be able to identify the brand as they consider and evaluate a selection of products and services, and when processing brand communication. Have you ever found yourself wanting to tell people about a really clever solution or a hilarious ad, but for the life of you can't remember which brand was the sender? You're not alone. It's worth remembering that unless people recognise and remember that your brand is behind the message, and that they find the message useful enough to start building a relationship with your brand over it, your investment will be wasted, regardless of how hard people laughed at your ad or how useful your stain removal tips were.
- Whether people buy the same product at the same place over and over, new products from the same brand, or same product in a different location, they'll have a set of *identical expectations* to the brand experience.
- Last but not least, the brand functions as something that people *identify with*. When we choose which brands we surround ourselves with, we are simultaneously saying something to our surroundings about who we are.

Communication

You may remember the linear communication models that illustrate communication as a sender, a message and a receiver? The key to understanding how important the brand identity actually is can be understood in light of these models. Kapferer's identity prism (2012, p. 158) can be read as a version of a slightly more complex type of communication models called transaction models. The transaction model includes the context in which the communication occurs. This means that factors such as the relationship between sender and receiver, cultural understanding – or misunderstanding for that matter – is taken into account when we try to understand the receiver's motivation to process the sender's message.

Our aim is to build brands that people want to include in their lives. A brand we understand, one that moves people and forges bonds can become an important part and welcome addition to people's lives. We trust Disney to provide us with family friendly entertainment in a way that's rooted in its long story telling history, but also to introduce new characters and stories that are relevant to our time. A brand that fails to understand the context in which it operates may overstep, become a comical figure that people give a wide birth to, ignore or avoid completely. Pepsi apologised for its portrayal of activists in a commercial after huge backlash from people who accused the brand of trivialising the issues (such as the killing of black men at the hands of the police, due to the brand's use of Black Lives Matter imagery in the ad) as well as the protesters' experience of police brutality. As the brand's spokesperson said: "Clearly we missed the mark and apologise" (New York Times 2017). The brand identity prism model is designed to take the environment in which a brand identity exists, and the influence of the one upon the other, very seriously.

The brand identity prism

How to use the prism

The brand identity prism is a tool that helps us understand the connection between the brand and the world in which it exists. The prism is best understood in light of a communication model where the brand is understood as the sender, the brand and the market/its customers exist in a common context, and the brand's target group is the receiver.

Using the identity prism model, you'll end up with a description of your brand identity as if it were a person, and the process forces us to consider each of the brand identity's facets. The brand identity prism may be the best-known of all of Kapferer's models. You'll find numerous examples of brand identity prisms online, ranging in quality from poor to pure genius. Which goes to show, the tool itself is no better than the person wielding it. While the identity prism may seem a bit complicated at first glance, it's well worth getting to know.

The brand identity prism structure

The prism is a hexagonal model divided into six parts. The three horizontal sections can be understood as a communication model: *the sender*, in this case the brand, *context*, in this case the shared world view of brand and customers, and *the receiver*, or the target group as it sees itself when interacting with the brand. The vertical line through the model separates the external from the internal.

The brand's physical traits

The first facet in the model is for the physical specificities and qualities that come to mind when people think of your brand. The name, your logo, a shape, a key product, the founder, a visible CEO, a spokesperson, a storyline, a tangible added value or objective feature of their home or office, a time of year or anything objective that seems to belong to a brand. When is, for example, your Dolmio day?

Every brand needs a physique so that people can know it when they see it. Sometimes the link between a brand's physical representation and its product category is very strong, particularly when it comes to market leader brands in mature industries.

We strongly associate the soda category with Coke. If we catch a partial glimpse of the logo, or even a weathered piece of Coca-Cola bottle glass, our thoughts go immediately to the brown fizzy drink, ice cubes and quenching of thirst. When people around the world find themselves fancying a cold soda, most of them will choose a Coke most of the time. And Coca-Cola makes sure to be within reach all over the world to benefit from the connection soda = Coca-Cola.

In order to be a visible sender, your brand needs a clear brand identity. In the olden days, sender identity in this context would refer to brand visibility on packaging and in advertising. Today, however, you want your brand to be recognisable in any dialogue in which it engages people, whether it's the user experience itself, contact with customer support or ideally also word of mouth as it passes from one customer to another. For this, you need a holistic design language more than a traditional visual toolkit, and you need a distinct and well defined verbal identity.

The brand's personality

A brand's personality is the personality customers, employees and other people identify with – or not. The simple question is: if this brand were a person, how would you describe his or her character?

Kapferer gives a word of warning against allowing this part of the brand platform to grow out of proportion, and the risk that your brand's unique personality could get lost in a sea of positive but generic character traits (2012, p. 172). The more people are involved and the number of iterations of the process to define your brand's personality, the greater the risk that clarity loses out to consensus. Agreement and general involvement can be good things, but it's worth keeping this risk in mind. To compete effectively you need a clearly differentiated brand, so do not compromise on clarity of character.

I bring it up at this point in the book because work with the brand identity facets tends to engage a lot of people. So sticking to our brand strategy perspective, please make sure you separate the character traits that belong to your category from the personality of your brand specifically.

Let's say your brand is a professional services brand. It goes without saying that you'll want your brand to be perceived as knowledgeable, professional and efficient. However, these are character traits that belong to the category. If any of these character traits are to be associated with a particular brand in the category, it must be because that brand gives the character trait a particular expression, represents it to a degree above and beyond the competition or exercises the trait in a unique way. There is a difference in the professionalism of a business lawyer and one that specialises in family law and it is that difference you must find a way to express as you work with this facet of the prism.

Relationship

The relationship facet of the prism addresses the intersection, and mode of interaction, between people and brand. The most important thing to remember when working with this facet is that what you're looking to define is the kind of relationship to which people are actually receptive. Too often brands aim to be: "a partner, not just supplier" or even "a friend". It's rare, however, to find customers who are willing to give your brand such an important role in their lives.

Consider Havas Media's study of global brands in Europe (Havas Meaningful Brands study 2015) for a moment. The study shows that three quarters of all brands might as well disappear and no one would mind one bit. Less than a third of the brands have people's trust and only one in ten brands contribute to people's lives in a positive way. However, the brands that are perceived as meaningful additions to people's lives outperform other brands on parameters such as stock value, ability to charge a premium and share of wallet. In other words, it's much better to establish a seemingly weaker, but more meaningful relationship to customers than to aim for some ideal out-of-reach kind of relationship.

The question is never what kind of relationship benefits the brand, but rather what kind of relationship is ideal for the customer. Is your brand a bit of sunshine on a grey afternoon, an innocent sin, a kind neighbour, a servant, a drill sergeant, a sweet seduction or a walking encyclopedia?

Over the years I have conducted a lot of research into people's relationships with various brands – primarily through interviews and other qualitative data gathering exercises. In my experience, people tend to be fairly precise in their descriptions, much more so than the brands' own spokespeople. One example where I was surprised at both the consistency and precision of people's responses was when we interviewed to discover what kind of relationship customers had to the Telia owned telecom brand MyCall. MyCall is targeted at immigrants and others looking for cheap long distance calls. Among this culturally diverse group of customers, many described the relationship to the provider that connected them with far-away family as family-like in itself. As in: MyCall is like a member of my family, a mother or sister, who looks out for me, makes sure I'm ok and helps me solve problems. Not bad for a telco!

Toms invites customers to join its "One for one" mission in other ways than giving away a pair of shoes for every pair sold. There's the "Ticket to give" campaign where people are encouraged to nominate friends, neighbours or family to join Tom's "Giving Trips". There's also an annual "Day without shoes" campaign to bring people on board to the cause by asking people to think about, and feel if only for a day, what it's like to live the life of one of the Toms shoes recipients.

If you're willing to agree that brands are built through relationships, you'll recognise that this facet warrants your attention. It's particularly important if your brand is in the services or low-engagement categories, or even categories where people relate to your brand often and over time, but without giving it much thought. It's much harder to replace a relationship than a product or service, especially if the products are more or less the same, such as electricity, broadband or phone subscriptions. In addition, understanding the customer brand relationship helps you make decisions about your brand's verbal identity (or which tone and style of communication to go for), channel choices, the expected level of personal service, response time and all the other things that when put together build a strong brand identity.

Culture

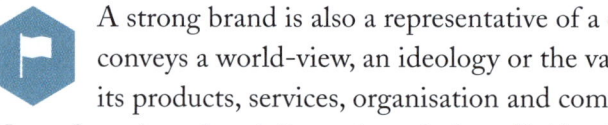

A strong brand is also a representative of a culture – it conveys a world-view, an ideology or the values that shape its products, services, organisation and communication. Very often, the cultural dimension of a brand's identity is rooted in the brand's origins or its creation myth, if you will.

This facet of the prism is not there to help you describe the internal culture of your business, although it too will be affected by the brand culture. What we are looking to describe through this facet is that which is shared, culturally, by the brand and its customers alike.

In Eurosport's recent rebrand it made a conscious decision to be explicit about the culture shared by the sports broadcaster and its audience – the sports fan culture. With its #sharemypassion social media campaign, it encourages fans to share stories about the extraordinary lengths they go to in order to demonstrate their love for their athlete, team or sport. Another consequence of the decision to drive this common culture element is manifest not only in advertising but also in its programming, now featuring more pre-match rituals and other elements that aim to capture that sense of excitement and tension. Less icons, less grandeur, more passion and more about the general ups and downs of sports and sports fandom.

Red Bull on the other hand belongs to a thrill seeking sub culture, whether we're talking about top athletes who dare to do things their own way, people who do extreme sports or just people who dream big and are willing to take risks to achieve them. Most people who drink Red Bull, probably feel like slightly bolder versions of themselves and may just push themselves a little bit harder. The Ben & Jerry's brand identity sits very comfortably within a hippie culture, where producing ice cream from the milk of happy cows in Vermont and sponsoring the Occupy movement are equally rad, man. It's interesting to note that this cultural dimension of the Ben & Jerry's brand has persisted and remains strong even after the acquisition by the great, global Unilever.

Understanding this cultural facet is particularly important when it comes to designing or updating visual and verbal profiles. Throughout the ages people have made use of colours, symbols, clothing, words and turns of phrase to express cultural identity. If a brand is very closely linked with a particular culture and/or the brand has a very close connection to its target group, any attempt to change or develop the brand identity's cultural facet must be done carefully and respectfully. A brand should not change its name or develop its identity beyond what its existing cultural dimension can tolerate with respect to how, when and how much. Understanding the culture of a brand's organisation is an important part of getting to the bottom of this. To shift a brand identity, you need a positive reason to do so, one that points towards some future position that's attractive to customers and employees alike.

According to Kapferer (2012, p. 159) the culture facet is the most important facet of brand identity, and the key to understanding the difference between brands is understanding that they are engaged in a cultural competition. He goes on to say that "brands are not only driven by a culture, but convey their culture" (2012, p. 159) and for great brands in particular, this new role as cultural champion provides new opportunities for strengthening and renewing their relationship with customers. Unilever as well as Coca-Cola engage in micro financing initiatives to help women in the developing world run small, local businesses. Thus, these brands spread an enterprising culture to the areas and introduce their products to new markets at the same time.

Taking Kapferer's new brand definition – a name with the power to influence – into account (Kapferer 2012, p. 8), it makes sense for him to have argued that it is through the cultural dimension brands find legitimacy for not only sharing in a culture, but actively taking steps to shape it, and the brand's role within the culture at the same time.

Reflection

The bottom part of the prism model is not so much about the brand as the people the brand exists for, whether they are customers, members, users, advocates or fans. The word refection in this context refers to reflection as if in a mirror, not reflection in the sense of pondering and reflecting upon the mysteries of the world. What we're talking about here is how the brand reflects upon its customers. To understand this facet, ask questions like: "What do people think about you as a user of this brand? What does using this brand say about you as a person?"

So, reflection in this sense is not about how most people view or judge users of a brand. Nor is it a way to define the brand's target group or audience. This facet addresses how users of the brand want to be perceived by people they care about. The difference may seem slight, but it's important. Consider very young girls with Louis Vuitton handbags for instance, whether knock offs or the real thing. It's fair to say that these girls are not the luxury brand's primary target group. Nevertheless, it's interesting to understand what these young girls want their LV handbags to say about them. What identity are they assuming? Is it a lifestyle they aspire to, would they like to be seen as grow up? Independent? Or is it something else that grown ups just don't get?

Which facet is most prominent will vary from brand to brand, but for any brand where the idea of being something to identify with is central, the refection facet will be extra important. For a brand like Harley-Davidson, for example, the reflection facet is crucial. Despite the fact that Harley-Davidson customers tend to be in the 40 plus demographic, with steady jobs and tidy lives, the customers bask in the rebellious light of the Harley-Davidson brand as it reflects upon them. We can imagine how an accountant with a Harley feels slightly less established – dare I say dull – than his fellow non-Harley-riding accountants. The brand speaks to how its target group wants to be seen, not as they are.

At one point, the British brand Burberry was almost hijacked when uncouth chavs adopted the brand in a very visible way, influencing the brand's reflection facet in a way not intended by the brand. In contrast, Adidas received unexpected help, becoming an almost overnight street wear icon, when adopted by the rap group Run-D.M.C. The group challenged the pop culture of the time by insisting on wearing on stage what they wore on the street – unlaced Adidas superstars. The street reflected on Run-D.M.C. and their star status reflected on the new Adidas wearers.

Uber, as mentioned earlier in the book with its original slogan *Everyone's private driver* used a clear reference to the attractive lifestyle of the stars, socialites, head honchos and others with too much to do and so little time in which to do it. Perhaps the reflection of this lifestyle was particularly attractive to the people of California where the first Ubers saw the light of day, as this is an area people who want to make it, whether as entertainers or entrepreneurs, gravitate towards.

Self-image

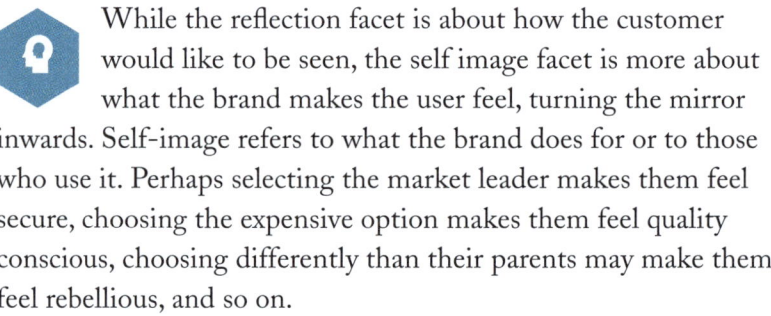

While the reflection facet is about how the customer would like to be seen, the self image facet is more about what the brand makes the user feel, turning the mirror inwards. Self-image refers to what the brand does for or to those who use it. Perhaps selecting the market leader makes them feel secure, choosing the expensive option makes them feel quality conscious, choosing differently than their parents may make them feel rebellious, and so on.

Questions to ask to make sure you fully grasp this facet are: "How do you feel when you buy/use/choose this brand? What is it about you that's accentuated when you use it? How does the brand impact how you feel about yourself?

Do girls that are presented with a Tiffany engagement ring feel just a little more loved than other girls? Are Tesla car owners proud of being simultaneously part of the solution to climate change and the owners of an awesome ride?

Again, when you're working to define the self-image facet of your brand's prism, be aware of our tendency to resort to descriptions that are generic to the brand's category. For example, when we read newspapers we feel more informed. But informed in what way? Do the readers feel that they have an overview of current affairs, or fully up to date on policy-making, or do they identify as in depth experts on all things Kardashian? Either way, newspaper brands must strive to represent themselves in response to customers' self-image so that they can more effectively make people understand that this newspaper brand is the one for me.

As it happens, customers are often better at defining this facet than people in the brand's organisation. It's all too easy for insiders to become blind to the nuances of this facet. So, it's worth asking people how they feel – while you're working to define your brand platform, but also when you think you're done, to check that it makes sense to people.

Process

As you now know, a brand platform consists of positioning, which you learn about in the positioning section of this book, and identity. It's usually a good idea to work at least somewhat in parallel on both elements of the brand platform. Prototyping a quick sketch of the brand identity prism can be a good place to start your entire branding process, as you're looking through the background materials and data available to you. As you sketch, you'll discover which of the facets are easy to define, as well as which facets seem more muddy. This discovery will save you the trouble of kicking in open doors, as well as directing your enquiry for further information. Knowing what you don't know means you can ask more specific questions when you interview customers and/or employees, in workshops and in any other part of the branding process. At the end of the day, your brand platform should go through some sort of validation, but initially, just finding out where you have clarity and agreement and where you don't can be very useful. It's particularly useful when it comes to the facets that touch upon relationship and culture. Actually, the same goes for poking around in the reflection and self-image facets as well, at the very outset if you can. Any customer satisfaction surveys, focus group results or polls you might have done will yield useful information if revisited and studied while wearing prism-goggles.

The prism is also well suited to the workshop format, whether the group is large or small. It works well with smaller management or project teams, or in "town halls" or other all-hands-on-deck kind of sessions if the entire organisation has been asked to contribute to the work of defining its future brand identity.

If you're workshopping the prism, it's helpful to make use of images, metaphors, comparisons and examples in addition to specific terms and description of your brand. To the extent that you have access to it, include competitor intelligence and insights about your industry and where it's going. Give examples of cases or customer testimonials that illustrate well what is special about your brand. It's possible to start with an empty prism and workshop it from scratch, but it's usually easier to ensure fruitful discussions if you start off with a pre-populated prism suggestion with which people can agree or disagree.

Clarity is rarely the result of identity-by-committee

Granted, the identity prism is not the simplest model to work with. It's a good idea to familiarise yourself with it by looking at prism examples of brands you already know well before bringing it in front of a large group. Again, I'd like to remind you of how easy it is to slip into consensus mode and end up with an image of something that's more appropriate to the category than it is to your specific brand within it. Here's the acid test: Ask yourself whether your prism might just as well be the prism of competitor A or competitor B. If so, start over.

When you're happy with the gist of your brand identity prism, make sure to boil it down. It should be possible to take in all six facets in one go and get an impression of a brand identity. Is this a role that's possible to play? Will the people in your organisation know how to act to make sure that your brand identity is expressed clearly and consistently? Everyone who works with the brand should be able to use the prism to understand what would be in line with the brand identity and what would not. It should help people feel confident about what to say and do in situations that have no specific manual for how to behave. It's much like the way an actor needs to understand a character to develop it and breathe life into it through the way it is acted out. Because there is no clear script for every situation and because the brand is built through the joint efforts of the many – brick by brick, customer by customer – the brand identity must be understood in the same way, or as close to the same as you can get, by everybody.

The brand identity prism gives expression to the brand's fundamental character and as such it will change very little. According to Kapferer (2012), the identity can only change in the sense that it develops with the times like any person can and still remain the same. The change must be in line with and respect the contract that made it attractive to customers in the first place. In contrast, positioning, which we discuss in the first part of this book, may change quickly and more often. A change in the competitive arena may require a change in a brand's differentiation strategy, or a brand may have to assume a new role due to market share growth or because it was replaced by a substitute. The identity, however, remains more or less constant. The rationale for why it must be so is the brand's role as replacement for the personal relationship between craftsman and customer and personal guarantee of a product's quality. Any person can – and will – change roles over time: from child to youth, from friend to lover, from colleague to mother to patient and so on, but the identity doesn't change much. So, while the identity prism must be reviewed and updated at regular intervals, it must be done gently and with respect for its history.

Everyday use

The identity prism is first and foremost a management tool that allows for decentralised decision-making. By that I mean giving people enough freedom and confidence to make decisions and communicate on behalf of the brand without strict manuals and fixed rules. This way, the prism becomes a source of creativity, new ideas and continuous improvement by helping people understand when a decision is right for the brand and when it is leading the brand astray. Never has this been more important than it is today.

In the new media reality, we know that everyone communicates with everyone, and that brands are built in everyday situations. Having a few people in your organisation and an ad agency that understands and knows how to express your brand identity is simply not good enough anymore. In practice, an organisation's management and marketing/communications departments will be the ones that know all the six facets of the prism like the back of their hands. For the rest of the organisation to come on board, the prism can benefit from further simplification. Instead of grappling with all six facets, understanding how to describe the following three will get you a long way: who *we* are (the top of the prism), who *they* are (the bottom of the prism), and what are the things we share (the middle part of the prism).

Simplified prism

Because the prism model is complicated, I will sometimes use a simplified version. When I simplify, I choose to overlook the difference between the internal and external perspective of the model, and boil it down to three questions.

What should people immediately associate with the brand?
It can be a colour, a product, a person or something else altogether. For most people Ferrari is red, Chanel is N° 5, and Nespresso is George Clooney.

What is the culture shared by the brand and the people it exists for?
It can be values, interests, a lifestyle or something else. If you enjoy Ben & Jerry's ice cream you may also think that same sex marriage is fine, of course love is love. Patagonia represents the call of the wild, while Moët & Chandon appeals to people with (or who wish they had) a glamorous life.

How does the brand impact how people who choose it feel about themselves?
Twitter likes its users to see themselves as participants in the global conversation, exercising their right to free speech. Tidal is a music streaming service aimed at people who see themselves as connoisseurs willing to pay a little bit more for the hifi experience of Tidal's lossless streaming service. Chanel wants to imbue a sense of timeless elegance in people who use it, so that they might feel as uniquely chic as Coco Chanel herself.

Regardless of whether you have the motivation to work your way through all the brand identity prism facets, or you need a quicker route to the destination, you'd do well to have ready answers to these three brand identity questions.

Simplified prism

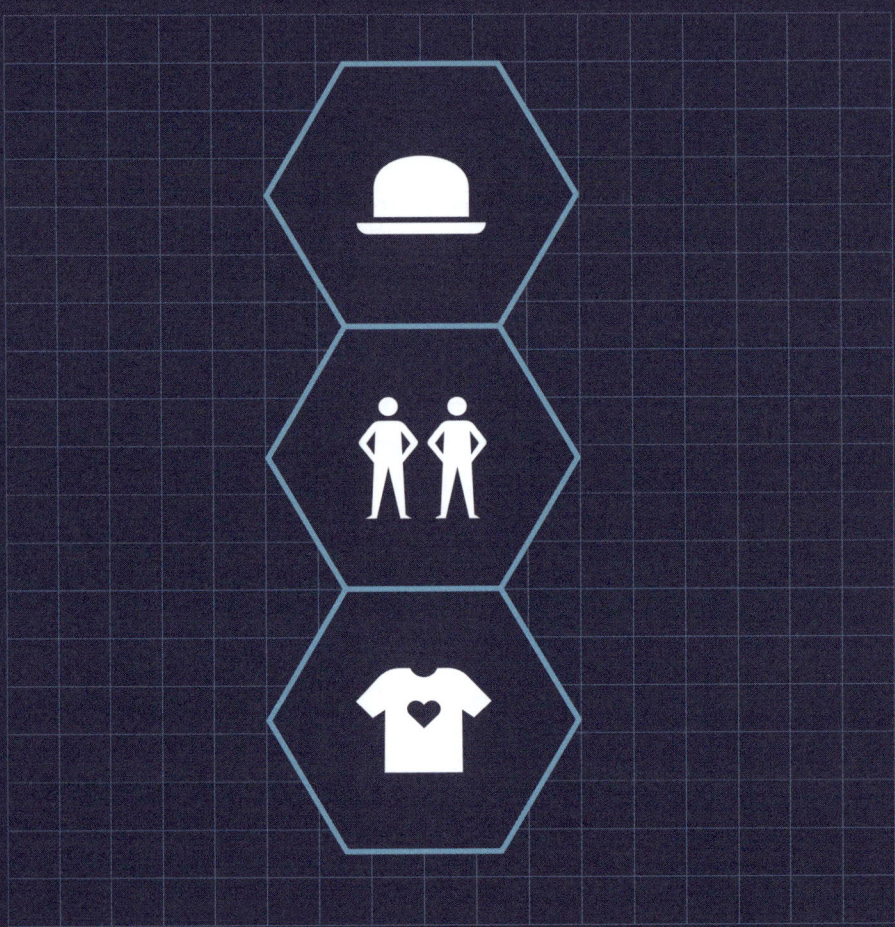

How to use the simplified prism

This is a simplified identity prism model. Sometimes it can be sufficient, or even necessary, to boil the rather complicated brand identity prism down to a more easily digestible format. Either way, working through the simplified model will give you valuable insight into the brand's identity, its culture and how it affects the people who choose it.

However your business chooses to communicate brand identity details internally, let this be very clear: a common understanding of your brand identity is a prerequisite if you want everyone in the organisation to act in accordance with it. If we think of the brand identity prism as a kind of character description for an actor, you might say that the closer the actor/employee is to the customers, the more they need to have the character under their skin. Nevertheless, each function of your organisation must be given the opportunity to interpret the brand identity as a character and decide how to play the part through the way their particular tasks are performed.

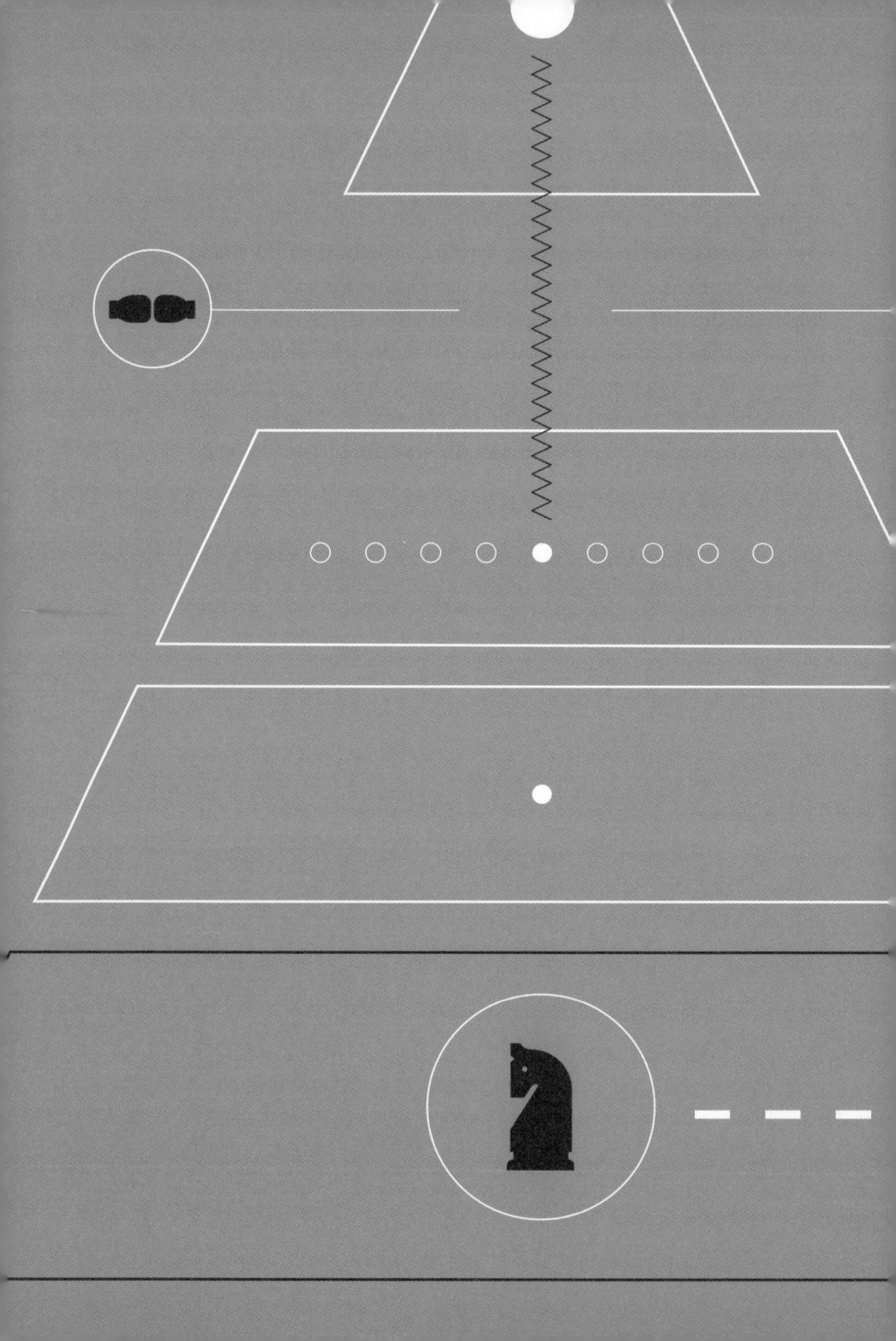

Strategic hierarchy

Integration

Strategic narrative

It's not difficult to put together a strategy; the difficulty is remembering where you put it

When you've got your brand platform sorted, its positioning as well as identity, you have a good description of your brand at its very best. You have defined clearly what your brand is, which role it plays in its market and how it's different from its competitors. You also have a clear description of who your brand is and to which human needs it appeals. Most importantly, you now understand clearly what kind of relationship you should aim to build between your brand and people, and you are sensitive to the values and in tune with the culture you share.

In and of itself this is pretty solid work. If you are, let's say, a management team or a group of entrepreneurs or a forceful communications department that has done the work together, you should already be seeing that more of your efforts and decisions are moving in the right direction.

But just like any other goal in life, it's more likely that you'll reach your branding goals if you have a plan. A brand platform embraced only by the marketing or communications department is necessarily less efficient than a brand platform that's fully integrated in the way your overall business strategy is communicated to and understood by everybody.

In the following section of the book, I'll introduce two tools to help you bring the entire organisation on board in the effort to realise your business' branding goals as a part of realising its business strategy. The first tool is a strategic hierarchy. In this context, the hierarchy functions as a short version of your brand platform and business strategy combined. The other tool is a strategic narrative, which is best understood as the story about how your brand and organisation play out their role in the market in order to achieve the chosen position. The strategic hierarchy and the strategic narrative are designed to help you mobilise everyone in the brand building effort as well as in realising your business strategy.

From burning platform to big opportunity

Just like the other tools and models you find in this book, the two integration tools stand firmly on both theoretical and academic legs. The tools are inspired by John Kotter's books. To a large extent, his work has set the standard for how we understand and talk about organisational change. Quite a few managers will be familiar with the burning platform concept and the unfreeze – change – refreeze phases of change management. However, in his book *XLR8*, released in 2014, Kotter performed a thorough review of what drives change and how that should impact our understanding of how to approach change as organisations and as management. The review was prompted by the same shift that's affecting the fundamental dynamics of business and brand management. It no longer makes sense to view our surroundings as inherently stable, interrupted from time to time by periods of change due to some extraordinary circumstance, before resettling into a new stable state. The premise of Kotter's review is that the market is in a continuous state of more or less fundamental change.

This way of understanding the normal state of markets led Kotter to revisit two of his change management concepts. Firstly, he reviewed the notion that an organisation needs to understand its present condition as some sort of crisis in order to be motivated to change; a burning platform scenario where it's obvious to everybody that the status quo is not an option. He found that it's simply too exhausting for an organisation to be constantly driven from one untenable situation to another, which in its turn is soon on fire and so on. Instead, Kotter pointed out the energy potential of a big opportunity. By pointing towards a big opportunity it's possible to create sufficient momentum to lead a transformation of your category, to usurp an attractive position from a competitor that's fallen asleep at the wheel, or to integrate a social purpose with your business model. If you're able to describe the new position – the big opportunity – as exciting and/or meaningful you're in a good position to bring about real change. You are, at least, in a much better position than you were managing an organisation in perpetual crisis mode, driven from one unsustainable position to the next.

For Bente Holm it was not exactly easy as the new head of the Oslo destination marketing organisation VisitOSLO, but it was easier to fire up the organisation to claim a digital pioneer position, than to motivate people by referring to demands made by a less-than-enthusiastic group of owners. She headed up a highly skilled organisation, but one that was skilled in the traditional ways of destination promotion. By being clear about what the organisation would do that was new and exciting going forward, rather than pointing out the old-fashioned things they would stop doing, she helped get the organisation to a place where it was both confident and brave enough to embrace the necessary transformation.

This new understanding of organisational change as a continuous rather than a three phased process (where the organisation's structures must first be dissolved, changed and finally re-solidified), makes it all the clearer how important the organisation's role in brand management has become. If the goal is to reach for a big opportunity, the brand should, to as great an extent as possible, support the organisation's efforts to influence the market, whether we're talking about customers, users, potential investors, staff, audience or authorities. The more people root for your chance to take advantage of the big opportunity, the greater the chance that it's you – and not your competitor – that actually get to do so.

Change is like riding an elephant

In the book *Switch* (2011) about how to change when change is hard, the brothers and academic writer duo, Dan and Chip Heath, make use of a wonderful metaphor of a rider and an elephant. To bring about change you need to make sure of three things; the rider must understand where he's going, the elephant must be motivated to stay on track and the road to the destination must be cleared.

In this picture, the rider represents the rational, the elephant the emotional, and the road is the process with all its intermediate objectives and decisions large and small. The elephant tends to choose the path of least resistance, particularly if it's unclear where it's headed or it's motivation to get there is low. And we all know who wins out if the head says one thing and the gut something else.

In light of this view of change, it should be obvious that a tool that everybody in the organisation understands and can use in their day to day decision making, that makes people feel confident that they are contributing to the realisation of the overall business strategy and that they do so in a way that strengthens the brand, must be a useful tool. We will give the rider direction and clear the path through the use of the strategic hierarchy tool. In addition, you need a powerful tool to motivate the elephant and that's what the strategic narrative is all about.

Chapter 7
The strategic hierarchy

A brand platform is no more useful than the results it helps realise. For that you need a strategy. However, just another strategy is the last thing most organisations need. Most organisations will have one already, one that management is already struggling to ensure reaches the whole organisation. Too often, the strategy will be difficult to understand even for highly motivated staff with a genuine interest in the future of the business. The greater picture can be hard to communicate regardless of whether an organisation's strategy is based on traditional Porter value chain theories or generic strategies, or you have set up a balanced score card system in line with resource based theory, or you're using newer models like Business Model Canvas. At the same time, businesses today need to make sure that innovation can – and does – happen at all levels and in all functions of the organisation. Top down initiatives will

It's not difficult to put together a strategy; the difficulty is remembering where you put it.

Willy Railo

Dr. Philos and professor in performance psychology

not be sufficient. It follows that making sure everyone in your organisation understands where you're going is not only useful, but necessary.

In their Harvard Business Review article (2008), Collis and Rukstad asked the rhetorical question, "Can you say what your strategy is?". As it turns out, even most executives can't. That being the case, it would be unfair to expect the rest of the organisation to defer to such a strategy when going about their day to day business. The solution proposed by Collis and Rukstad comes in the form of "A hierarchy of Company Statements": which, when all is said and done, is very similar to what I call a strategic hierarchy. A strategic hierarchy is made up of the usual strategy development elements organised as a hierarchical pyramid. It shows how the strategy elements are organised according to a logical principle, placing business strategy within a larger, more holistic, context.

Organisations that have this kind of overview of the hierarchy of its most central tenets, and also use it actively in its brand development, effectively make brand development an integrated part of its business strategy and as such everybody's business.

Over the years I have noted that organisations that make active use of such a one-page strategy overview seem to be more successful than those that don't, and this seems logical. An at-a-glance overview of a company's purpose and its goals and strategies that's given high visibility within an organisation is a much more effective management tool in an ever changing world than any key performance indicator, score board or benchmark can ever be.

The bridge between your business strategy and brand platform

Brands have been seen most of all as marketing vehicles. With that perspective it may not be altogether clear how motivating your organisation to deliver on its business strategy and its brand are connected. Similarly, it's not always clear to people why communication or marketing departments would need a strategic hierarchy. Luckily, it's usually the case that when a management team has committed to a clear description of a brand in the form of a brand platform, they usually also understand the benefit of integrating the brand in the day to day operations. One important business strategy decision is, in fact, to define the role and impact of branding.

This chapter is for those who see the benefit of assigning an important role to branding, and we'll look into how a hierarchy of strategy tenets can include the brand perspective in a good way. I'll start by saying something about the hierarchy as a whole, brand perspective included, before moving on to each of the elements that make up the strategic hierarchy pyramid.

- Maintain your outside-in perspective in shaping and formulating the strategic hierarchy. Just as it should be possible for employees, owners and other stakeholders to understand and subscribe to a specific strategic choice for your brand, they should also understand, and want to stand behind, your strategic hierarchy.
- Stand on top of your brand platform as you create your strategic hierarchy. It is a platform after all. In practice, this means that while your business strategy is the parent of your brand strategy, your brand platform will and should influence the way your strategic hierarchy is written and presented. If, let's say, your brand is to be a challenger in its category,

there are rules that must be followed for your brand to be understood as a challenger. One such rule, or clear expectation connected to the challenger role, is that the challenger stands out as a clear and differentiated alternative to the category's market leader. A successful strategic hierarchy for a challenger brand should therefore be designed and formulated based on a thorough understanding of the market leader's strategy and identity. The market leader brand on the other hand, must make sure its strategic hierarchy includes the necessary measures to allow it to stay ahead and keep moving the category forward.

- Look to find or create turns of phrases that have energy and that can take on a life of their own within the organisation. In my experience, for the organisation's mission, goals and strategies to come to life among your people, the words that describe them must do the same. The statement "We are Oslo Boosters" is easier to remember and live by than "We are a customer centric organisation and measure our success on the value we create for our stakeholders". Don't be afraid to let energy take precedence over precision here. As long as you have a management willing to use the hierarchy actively, the precise meaning of the words expressed in it and how they are connected will be clear to everybody soon enough.
- Keep it practical. Discussions about what a vision or a mission *really* is rarely lead to ground-breaking insight. Over this long journey, throughout which I have picked up the tools presented in this book, I have learnt at least one thing for sure. Definitions are far less important than coining phrases that are used and understood. So, if you end up with a strategic hierarchy that gives direction and is meaningful to people, who cares if the pyramid is or isn't completely by the book? If you find one or some of your hierarchy elements are not 100

per cent according to their theoretical framework definition, but they work for you, there's no doubt in my mind what will have to give. Steve Job's wish to make a dent in the universe is easy to understand and contains a huge amount of energy. But is a mission or a vision? And does it matter?

The elements of the pyramid

Deciding on the order in which to present the elements of the pyramid is not easy. In practice, you work them out much as you would a jigsaw puzzle. Some pieces fall into place almost by themselves right away. Once you have placed the first pieces, you see where the next ones go. Just as with jigsaw puzzles, it can be a good idea to start with the outer edges. For your strategic hierarchy, that would be the top and bottom of the pyramid.

Mission on top

In this book, we start at the top with your undertaking, the "why you exist" of your business, also called your quest, mission or purpose. According to Collis and Rukstad the mission "spells out the underlying motivation for being in business in the first place – the contribution to society that the firm aspires to make" (2008). An even simpler description of what a mission should contain is as follows: "Who we are, what we do, and why we are here" (Thompson et al. 2012).

The mission's job is to make clear why the organisation behind a brand does what it does. Very often organisations in the same category will also have quite similar mission statements. Any insurance company is about alleviating risk, a clothing brand makes clothes through which people express their identity or that enable their lifestyle. Organisations, companies, and brands that seem driven by an idea that's greater than its business idea however, tend to have a mission statement that stands out, especially if that idea is manifest in the statement. Toms mission is a good example. The business started with shoes, but when the mission is simply to *improve lives* (Toms 2016) there's nowhere the brand can't go. The brand can extend to any product category where Toms *one for one* principle can apply. The skip from shoes to eyewear and next, a hop to rucksacks are easy transitions for the brand and in line with the organisation's ethos and culture.

The most important feature of a mission is that it is clearly understood by employees, customers and other stakeholders. All further decisions, especially decisions concerning what is within and outside the scope of your business, derive from its mission. In our day and age when categories, technologies and business models are constantly changing, it's more useful to have a mission statement that describes what you want to achieve, than one that describes what you produce.

In practice, the difference between your mission and your business idea may be mostly semantic. However, business ideas are often defined along the lines of "what we offer to whom in which unique way," which makes it a little too concrete for the most inspiring mission statements.

Brand considerations kick in, in several ways, when it comes to the actual wordsmithing of your mission statement. Your brand's role in the category, the kind of relationship it has with its customers and the impact as perceived by your customers of choosing your brand, should all guide your work on this. A dominant market leader brand may clearly take responsibility for the category and the entire category's environmental footprint or contribution to society. A pioneer – or an established brand that wants to bring back the pioneer within – will often have a mission that's all about effecting some sort of change.

Below, you will see a few mission statement examples. Now that you know how these organisations define what they're looking to contribute to the world, you can take a moment to reflect upon how these statements affect your desire to connect with them.

General Electric: GE's mission is to invent the next industrial era, to build, move, power and cure the world. (GE, 2016)
Kickstarter: Our mission is to help bring creative projects to life (Kickstarter 2017)
Google: Google's mission is to organize the world's information and make it universally accessible and useful. (Google 2016)
Chanel: To be the Ultimate House of Luxury, defining style and creating desire, now and forever. (Chanel 2017)
Tesla: To accelerate the world's transition to sustainable energy. (Tesla 2017)
Microsoft: Our mission is to empower every person and every organisation on the planet to achieve more. (Microsoft 2017)

Values or fundamental beliefs

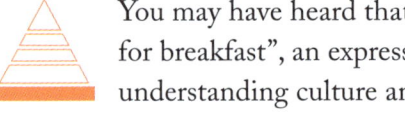
You may have heard that "culture eats strategy for breakfast", an expression of how important understanding culture and its values is to strategy processes. (The saying has no documented source, but is usually attributed to Peter Drucker.) Traditionally, "values" in this context has been understood as internal, as if referring to the organisation's culture. Increasingly, however, it's also a question of shared values – the common culture of the organisation and its stakeholders.

I have come across organisations that have approached the question of values with a thoroughness that has resulted in expressions of its organisation's culture at its best. I have also come across businesses that have had engaging value processes that may have raised the energy level there and then, but that have not been able to bring any sustained or meaningful benefit over time. Very often, I find that people are weary, some times to the point of outright resistance, of revisiting this topic. But there's no reason to treat this part of the pyramid any differently than the other parts. Either the organisation's management will already know or relatively easily be able to come up with the content. Or the values can be decoded from internal and external insights utilised for the brand strategy process and presented as a suggested values statement that management should be able to recognise as valid. Should neither of these avenues lead to a clear understanding of the values that define the culture and/or underpins the customers' bond with your brand, your organisation has a bigger problem, which is outside the scope of this book. In practice, it's usually not that hard to get there.

Regardless of how you proceed to define your values statement, once you have it, make sure everybody takes it to heart so that it informs people's day to day decisions: how they behave towards each other and customers as they go about realising your joint mission successfully.

Your values statement as the foundation of your strategic hierarchy

Your values form the foundation from which your mission is born. This foundation explains why your organisation does what it does; it explains why it has taken upon itself to contribute to the world in such or such a way, and puts into context why the organisation is made up in a certain way to be able to deliver on its mission. This values-derived foundation tends to be very important to the organisation's culture in that it defines a right way to view the world, in many ways becoming a guide to a particular way of thinking and acting.

So what does a values statement look like? There's no template. As long as it is formulated in such a way as to clarify what's important enough to the organisation to make it what it is and do what it does, it's a values statement. You'll probably find it in the anecdotes people share or phrases they repeat – stories or expressions that tend to pop up in connection with important decisions, particularly when decisions must be made quickly or with an uncomfortable degree of uncertainty. In those circumstances, it's nice to be able to rest on what the organisation really believes, stands for and shares with its customers. The decision may turn out to be the wrong one but at least it was made for the right reasons.

VisitOSLO had a new understanding about what it would take to bring more people to the city, and the organisation felt so strongly about it that it felt necessary to codify this new understanding in its values statement: *More and better stories about Oslo lead to more and better stories about Oslo.* The rationale behind this sentence is the recognition that people check with friends, acquaintances, blogs, journalists' reviews and curated best-of lists, when deciding where to travel, how to stay and what to do when they get there. VisitOSLO can only influence these sources to a very minor degree, considering the amount of information already out there. However, by helping people who have already decided to travel to Oslo, or who live in Oslo, to use the city more and share their experiences, that information will reach more people who may in turn decide to come. VisitOSLO really believes that this is the way to go and it influences the way the organisation goes about realising its mission in a fundamental way. Also, when at times it feels tempted to revert to the traditional ways of destination marketing, this values statement helps the organisation hold fast to its new ways and not look back.

Also – Google's philosophy summed up as the well known *Don't be evil* is as good a values statement as any.

Values that are truly valuable

I once read an article about values where the author claimed that for a value to be a true core value in an organisation it has to be such a strong part of the culture that acting contrary to it makes your stomach ache – that you'd rather change category than abandon the value. I've not been able to track down the source of this description, but it's stuck with me over the years because it describes the role of values so succinctly.

The point of defining clear values is exactly that. To make sure that everybody in the organisation (potential new employees included) knows what's valued highly enough that it sets clear boundaries for choices and actions, in terms of both which behaviour is rewarded even if there may be a financial cost in the short term, and which behaviour is frowned upon or even sanctioned even if initial results seem positive.

It's common for organisations to set highly generic values – such as integrity, excellence, teamwork and similar. These kinds of values probably feel safe if the main purpose of defining values is having, and being able to refer to, a set of values. If they are repeated often enough in an organisation they may also lead people to feel they know what's expected of them as a result. But why this tendency toward the general? Would any organisation survive that has no integrity, that is more than happy with poor performance and that fails to work together as a team?

Values that live in strategy documents alone and that have not been adopted by the culture, have very little power. I'll just mention here that Enron's values were respect, integrity, communication and excellence.

A company's practices and strategies should change continually; its core ideology should not.

Collins and Porras

Building Your Company's Vision, Harvard Business Review, 1996

How to define valuable values

For organisations that have clear values that are already embedded in its culture there's no reason to drag people through a process to define those values all over again as a part of putting together a strategic hierarchy. However, if an organisation has no expressed values or its values are terribly generic, the following checklist may be helpful:

1. Look for values that have been important to your organisation from its very beginning. The values that stem from the origin of your business will often be connected to its mission in a profound way, explaining why it goes about realising its mission in a certain way. These are values that tend to also resonate with your target groups' values.

2. Look for values that are already strong, or at least latent, in your culture and that will be particularly important to the organisation in the future, both in order to reach certain goals but also to ensure that the strategies meant to take you there are actually executed.

3. And last but not least: look for values that are particular to your organisation – something that means more to you than it does to your competitors. It could be values derived from your chosen positioning (role in particular), archetype (or what really motivates people to bond with your brand), a target group you're looking to attract, or something else altogether.

Select the values that are truly the most important and formulate a statement that makes your values easy to remember and talk about.

Th

nk

Semantics and pragmatics

An organisation's values don't have to be values in the strict grammatical sense. Whatever feels crucially important to an organisation, that which it takes pride in being when it's being its very best, *that* is a value in this context.

My two favourite examples are IBM and Apple. Throughout the years *Think* has been a core value at IBM. It was important enough that Thomas J. Watson, legend and leader of IBM for many years, had a plaque of the word Think on his desk. When a poor soul came to present to the big boss, the plaque was right there in his or her face as a reminder of exactly what was expected. The word itself, think, set a wonderfully aspirational tone for people who wanted to make a real difference and play an active part in the early days of the computer era.

IBM also illustrates well that one good core value can be enough and have longevity. When IBM did not see open standards coming early enough, and miscalculated the speed of growth in the personal computer market, it became a shadow of its former glory for a while. Nevertheless, Think remained and was adopted by new management looking to take the business in new directions. Think was exactly the right core value for a business reinventing itself for a new time.

Apple's *Think different* challenge to IBM and PCs is well known. It was a bold move from a tiny rebel challenger at the time, showing all the gutsy attitude of the two young college dropouts in the now famous Silicon Valley garage. Later on, getting "stewed" by Steve Jobs, and in no uncertain terms being told to think more differently, became almost a badge of honour. In the years after Steve Job's death in 2011, critical voices have asked whether Apple has become too predictable. It remains to be seen whether Tim Cook, the current Apple CEO is able to inspire the organisation to think different going forward, or whether Apple will be challenged in its turn by new players driven by inspiring core values of their own.

Overarching goals

The overarching goals are there to show the organisation that it's on track towards achieving its mission and realising its vision. From a brand perspective, it's important that the goals also reflect the role the brand plays in the competitive arena and that its differentiated position shines through.

When setting appropriate goals for your strategic hierarchy, it's useful to juxtapose its mission and its values statement and ask the question: "Given that this is what we believe (the values statement), what are the clearest indicators that we are on track towards achieving this (the mission)"?

The juice and smoothie company Innocent has an outsourced produce strategy, meaning that they buy rather than grow the fruit and vegetables that go into its drinks. The company is well aware that the fruit and vegetable business can be a dirty one and has taken a clear stand on modern slavery, listing its various initiatives to mitigate the risk of any of its suppliers ignoring its human rights policies. The overarching goal is for there to be no kind of modern slavery, child labour, or people trafficking occurring in any part of its supply chain. Simply stating this as a goal is nowhere near enough. Measures and initiatives, from whistleblowing procedures to auditing and investment in human rights projects, keep the company on track as to how it's doing against this clear and ambitious overarching goal.

For VisitOSLO, being able to refer to its overarching goals helped the organisation demonstrate to its stakeholders that generating results for them is core to fulfilling VisitOSLO's mission – namely growth in the experience and hospitality industries in Oslo. Not only was the organisation undergoing massive change, but the decision to assume the role of a digital pioneer organisation itself entailed doing new and unfamiliar things. It's not unusual for opposing interests or mutually excluding priorities to come up. How quickly do we let go of the old way of doing things and what is our capacity for experimenting with the new? How do we distribute our resources, human as well as financial? When you have set a couple of overarching goals, each with its clear call to action, dilemmas like these become easier to navigate. One goal (We'll make being a good host worthwhile!) was a clear signal to the organisation that VisitOSLO's job, and the responsibility it has towards its various stakeholders – visitors to Oslo, the city's cultural scene, entertainment industry and its hospitality industry – is to increase their stakeholders' revenue. Only then will the job have been done successfully. The other goal (Increase Oslo's digital footprint) measures whether VisitOSLO has been able to successfully encourage people to share their Oslo stories. The digital footprint increase could come as a result of more people visiting the city, or as a result of more of the people who visit telling Oslo stories in social media or other digital channels. When we see an increase both in revenue (that hospitality actually pays) and the digital footprint, we have an indication that the values statement – in which the organisation believes – holds water. That when people share their Oslo stories, people are in fact inspired to come and have Oslo experiences and their stories in turn inspire new people to visit and make use of what the city has to offer.

A kind of checklist

Organisations rarely have a shortage of goals. However, the trick here is to define a couple, or a very few, goals that are truly overarching. It can be a good idea to shelve the existing list of key performance indicators and targets to begin with for the sake of encouraging open discussion rather than simply a prioritisation exercise juggling the same old items all over again.

- Look to identify goals that connect the values and the mission. Such as: because we believe this, and we have set out to contribute with this, these goals will be good indicators that we are headed in the right direction.
- First decide what your goals are, then find out how to measure whether you are achieving them. Going in the opposite direction, taking something you're already measuring as your stating point is just silly. But make no mistake, until you have found a way to discover to what extent your goals are actually being achieved, you are not finished setting goals.
- The goals must make sense to everybody: owners, employees, customers and society at large. In practice, most people will not be too interested in your overarching goals or your strategic hierarchy for that matter, but it's a great advantage if anyone that might take an interest could take a look, understand and approve of your way of thinking.
- And last but not least, focus on the big picture. We are easily influenced by owners' demands for profitability, or interests that some sort of internal perspective be given the prominence of an overarching goal. The goals must be defined in such a way as to be able to do their job within the strategic hierarchy and their job is to act as signposts along the way to let you know that you are practicing your mission

The strategic hierarchy - VisitOSLO

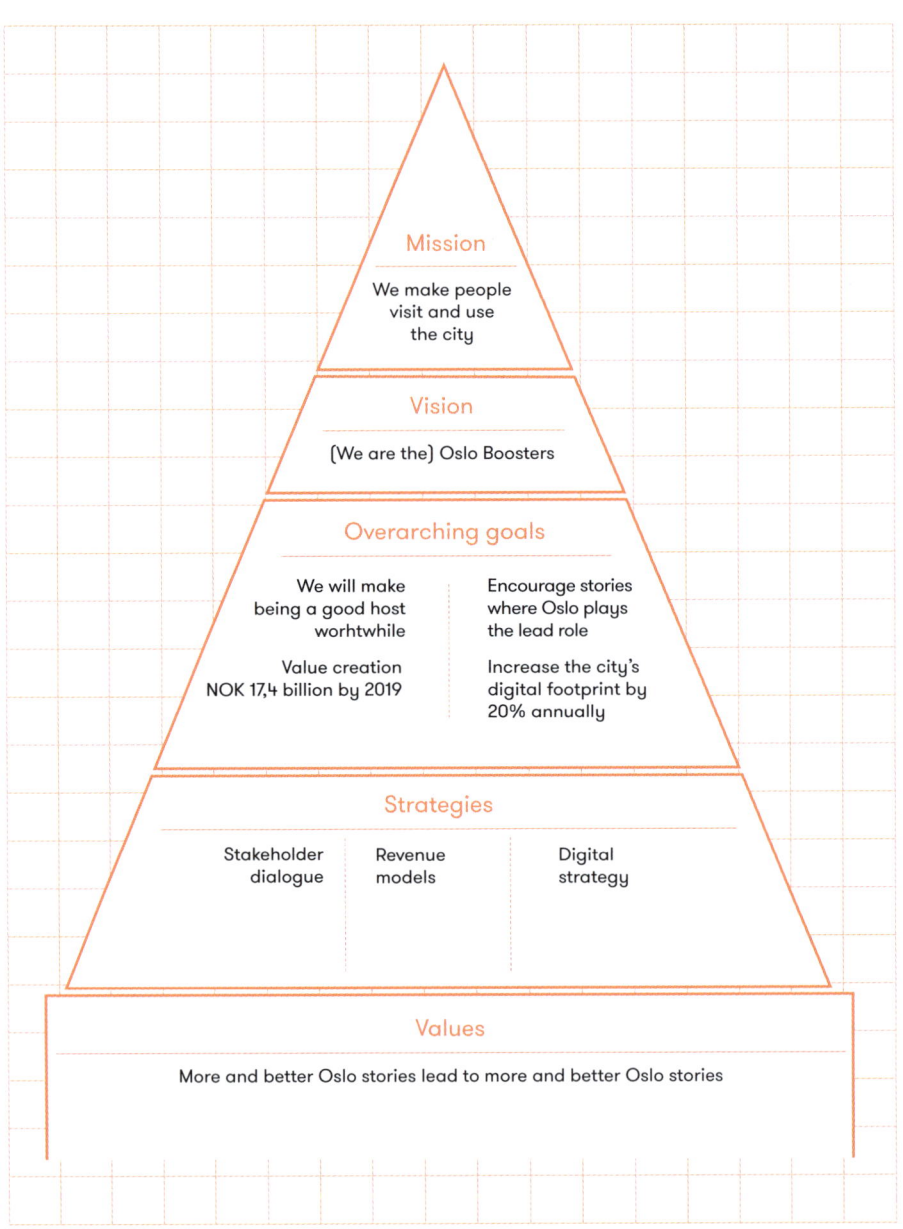

in accordance with your values. In addition, goals that are more operational in nature become easier to understand in the light of the overarching ones.

Strategies

In our time, when the winds of change are constant, organisations and management teams alike require frameworks that help them seize opportunities in the competitive arena as well as avert or deal with threats. If your business becomes too nimble, however, your change competence may come at the expense of a discernible strategic direction. For most businesses, the really big decisions remain fairly stable. And it's navigating between one big decision and the next that requires an almost constant ability to adapt. Whenever circumstances call for changes in one or several of your most central strategic choices, it helps if the organisation can follow the rationale for why change is necessary. Being familiar with the integrated whole of the strategic hierarchy puts them in a position to do so.

The strategies defined in the strategic hierarchy lay out your plan for what it will be necessary to do in order to reach the overarching goals. While operational efficiency is measured by the result of your various activities, the strategies defined here are all about finding a pattern where your business' qualities, assets and efforts combine in such a way as to lead to lasting competitive advantages. Your competitors may try to align with one or several of your strategies, but they'll struggle to copy the entire pattern.

These strategic choices, outlined in your hierarchy, form the strongest link between your brand and your business strategy. For example, how will the different grocery shops respond to the rapid growth of meal kit delivery services and online food shopping in general? And what will petrol stations become in the future considering how we are already just popping in there to get coffee while the car is charging?

That's why it is in this part of the strategic hierarchy the magic happens – clear strategic choices that mobilize the entire organisation to move forward in the same direction.

Strategy and the platform

Remember that this is exactly how your brand platform was designed as well – built in its entirety through a series of clear choices. "We will compete in this category, we will assume such and such a role, these are our differentiation criteria and we are different in exactly this way, this is how we will appear and this is the kind of relationship we aim to build with this set of customers". The same thing is true for your brand strategy and your business strategy: not everything can be equally important. By the same logic, only the most critical components of a brand and business strategy find their way into this pyramid.

For example, you might say that when BrewDog entered the "competition" to brew the world's strongest beer in 2009 with the Nuclear Tactical Penguin clocking in at 32 per cent alcohol, the move was motivated by its brand building potential rather than the market potential of the beer itself. Since then, other providers of artisanal beers have signed up to the competition and BrewDog has upped the ante with Sink the Bismarck (41 per cent) and End of History (55 per cent). While important to the branding effort, staying ahead in this particular competition may not warrant a place among the strategies of the strategic hierarchy.
On the other hand, having a beer in all the expected categories – IPA, lager, Weiss bier, stout etc. - which belong to the bottom of

the differentiation rocket as something you just have to do to be an artisanal beers provider, will be important to brand and business alike and thus require a designated strategy to make sure the beers are brewed and named and distributed.

So, as you define the strategies for your hierarchy, consider what it is that your business does that's different, or does in a different way compared to your competitors. To do this successfully, you'll need to look at the bigger picture again, your choices here cannot be derived from your business strategy, or as expressions of your brand as such. They must be borne out of the greater context of the combination of the two.

To reach our goals we must…
To get the right strategies for your hierarchy ask the following question: "As a result of which strategic choices will we most effectively reach our overarching goals in a way that's in line with our values"?

One way to formulate such a strategy is to include what it covers, or its *scope*, which *choice* has been made and an indication of how the organisation will *act* as a consequence of that choice.

Here, just like across the entire pyramid, there are no extra points for correct strategy speak. The important thing is that people understand that choices have been made, what the choices are and that they are to be followed no matter what.

Which strategies and how many?
Most businesses will have working strategy documents and a clear set of choices pertaining to "the shop". The purpose of the strategic hierarchy is to make the most important choices visible and transparent to everybody, even when they change. There are two

The difficulty lies, not in the new ideas, but in escaping from the old ones

John Maynard Keynes

The General Theory of Employment, Interest and Money, 1936

reasons why that's important. First, you want people to know what your strategic choices are so that they can act accordingly. Secondly, you want people to understand what it is about these choices that makes your business what it is. With the current pace of change around us, at least it's easier to deal with change and adopt various initiatives when people understand how they are prioritised, or not, in line with predefined strategies. The difference is much like the difference between a firecracker, which sends its energy in every which direction, and a precise shot moving with all its energy towards a target.

In practice, we usually end up with 5-6 clearly formulated main strategies. This is probably as many strategies as people can comfortably keep top of mind and actually use to guide their day to day choices and to make sense of the choices made by colleagues.

To inform your work on this part of the pyramid, it can be helpful to hang everything you've got – all the business strategy stuff as well as the materials that guided your brand platform process – up on a wall. Compare, and select the most important decisions that everyone should be aware of. Finally, look for sayings or expressions that are already in use – formally or informally – when people talk about strategy.

If you don't find these expressions, make up suggestions that you think will resonate with your culture.

When you have a good line up of well formulated strategies, this part of your pyramid is done. And by that, I don't mean that it will replace your dynamic and on-going strategy work, but that this part of the pyramid is now ready to function as a kind of map showing the general lay of the land.

Vision

Saving the vision for last can be a good idea. By then, the rest of your pyramid will have found its form and you can concentrate on the missing piece – the thing that joins all the elements together and infuses your entire strategic hierarchy with the energy required to realise its potential. That is the vision's job.

One question always comes up when we work with this, so I'll address it right away. The question is: why doesn't the vision belong at the top of the pyramid? The answer is simple. The mission gives us the purpose, why the organisation exits, the mission is in fact the justification for its existence. This cannot be subordinate to even the most energizing vision.

The vision is an image of the organisation at its very best, or of the world as it looks when the organisation has fully realised it mission. Whatever formulation of a vision that motivates people to move in the right direction, that's the right formulation of your vision.

The most exciting approach to formulating a vision comes from the Harvard Business Review article "Building Your Company's Vision" (Collins and Porras 1996). In short, and not entirely precise, their approach is to think of the vision as one part ideology and one part image of the future. The ideology is determined and defined by the organisation's mission and values. The future image should be a vibrant description of what the world looks like when the organisation has realised a BHAG – Big Hairy Audacious Goal.

In practice, the vision has a tendency to simply materialise at some point in the process. It can be useful to take advantage of someone with a particular knack for words, but the most important thing is that the vision is expressed in such a way as to be meaningful and rousing – most importantly of all perhaps is that it is energizing to the CEO, who more than anyone else is expected to champion the vision. The acid test is this: Will the top person in your organisation proudly give expression to this vision and be energized by it? And will it move and excite your people? If not – work on it some more.

Here's a few examples – which ones would you be able to express with enthusiasm?

IKEA: To create a better everyday life for the many people. (IKEA, 2017)
NASA: We reach for new heights and reveal the unknown for the benefit of humankind. (NASA, 2017)
Facebook: Bring the world closer together. (Facebook, 2017)
Amazon: Our vision is to be earth's most customer centric company; to build a place where people can come to find and discover anything they might want to buy online. (Amazon 2016)
LEGO: Inventing the future of play. (LEGO 2016)

How do you do it?

Unfortunately, there's no fixed playbook. I've had clients spend anywhere from 4 hours to 18 months on a first draft of their strategic hierarchy. Needless to say, these clients approached the pyramid at different stages of their strategy and/or branding processes and in very different circumstances. In one instance, which included a very large organisation wanting to include the whole organisation in every step of a fundamental turnaround process, this was critically important to the success of the undertaking.

> " A really good strategic hierarchy is one that helps everybody in the organisation find the most direct path to the destination, which means "easy to understand" wins every time.

The first example refers to Bente Holm and the destination promotion brand VisitOSLO. In this case, she not only headed up a small and nimble organisation, but the kinds of changes the organisation wanted to push through were already understood and approved by board, owners and other stakeholders.

This serves to illustrate that other processes taking place in your organisation in parallel will influence your work with the strategic hierarchy. If I may give you one recommendation it's this: separate content and its expression. By that I mean, work separately to define what each item should say, and next how that content should be expressed. It's all too easy to get bogged down in semantics or get caught up in the eagerness to be catchy too soon. The real decisions here are about the substantive content. Wordsmithing is usually not committee work anyway, and is best left to someone who has a way with words, once the substance has been decided.

As you work your way through all the elements of the pyramid, gradually place what you have into the whole and you will discover how the different elements support each other and can check that it actually works as a whole. When you decide that it does, that's the time for crafting the actual text to express it. And remember, meaningful trumps both poetic and precise when it comes to these formulations. A really good strategic hierarchy is one that helps everybody in the organisation find the most direct path to the destination, which means "easy to understand" wins every time.

Based on this very high level strategic hierarchy it will now be possible to lay plans and set targets for all the strategies, and ensure that you have processes in place to nurture and strengthen your values. A strategic hierarchy should have enduring value over time. It will be supported by short term action plans that change more frequently. However, should your positioning change, you will want to revisit your strategic hierarchy as well. If, for example, you are a challenger brand that overtakes the market leader, or perhaps something happens to fundamentally shift the competitive arena, or (which sometimes also happens) the world view that supports your values statement no longer seems relevant, then rethinking your strategic hierarchy becomes important.

Chapter 8
Strategic narrative

Include everybody in the branding efforts

Some products or services, companies or organisations, tend to pop up in everyday conversation, while others only get our attention if hit by some sort of scandal. When John Lewis releases its Christmas advert, that in itself is news. Similarly, it's hard to say what's more exciting to talk about after Super Bowl – the sports or the latest Budweiser commercial. Lately, Uber's battle against taxi companies around the world has come up on many people's radar.

Becoming a brand people pay attention to, have an opinion about and perhaps even root for has great value. In his book *True Story* (2013), Ty Montague shows us how businesses that have a compelling story that is conveyed through its actions, perform better than those that don't have any awareness of such a big story to guide their actions. It's also interesting to note that another benefit of having such a big story is manifest in that these companies' media and marketing spending is much lower than that of the others.

Before I became aware of the arguments made in *True Story*, my colleagues and I would usually go directly from defining and documenting the brand platform to implementation mode. We would start by identifying and developing which measures, both practical and symbolic, could kick start the process of change. But we'd also get into the nitty gritty of a step by step brand implementation process, such as developing a visual identity (if the existing profile no longer fits), a verbal identity (if the organisation needs a more distinct voice, a cause or an aspiration), action plans and all kinds of brand roll out activities large and small. And that's worked quite well. As a general observation however, when it comes to branding, just like any other business discipline, getting real world benefits from your strategy development efforts goes much smoother in organisations that have a culture that's comfortable with change and where management speaks its mind clearly.

The missing tool in the box was one that could help point out the expected results of the strategy when implemented and also to mark the transition to the implementation phase. This has been a bit of a missing link – the piece of the puzzle to make it easier for those who have developed the strategy to bring everybody on board to realising it. And that's what the strategic narrative does. This is a chapter about telling big stories.

Short stories and long stories

People have been telling each other stories since the beginning of time, way back when a dark cave wall was considered a suitable media channel (Monarth 2014). We told each other stories about ancestors, stories that cemented social norms, gave advice on how to manage the forces of nature and keep the gods happy. The stories played a crucial part in transferring knowledge from one generation to the next. Who could say the same about your average annual report?

That storytelling works when it comes to influencing consumers to buy certain products has been a celebrated fact at least since the golden age of advertising in the 1950s and 60s. When the VW Beetle was introduced to the US market, it was done in contrast to all the conventional stories told to make cars attractive to people at the time. With ads like "It makes your house look bigger", "Think Small" and perhaps most famously, the ad showing the round little car together with one word - "Lemon" - a term usually reserved for beat up old vehicles with all sorts of issues. The stories about the beetle were stories of an affordable and practical car in a category that had been dominated by stories that were mainly about how to increase your social status.

The influencing power of storytelling is well known and much used by politicians, business leaders and is one of the standard weapons in any communications advisor's arsenal. The entertainment industry has taught us that an episode, or even a scene, can be exciting in itself, but that it's even better to have people hooked on a grand epic that maintains their interest over time, creating expectations and anticipation as to how the story will unfold even when we all know how the story goes. In a romantic comedy, we know that the lovers will unite in the end and if it's a murder mystery, we expect that the killer will be revealed.

And it's precisely this kind of dramatic composition the story telling aspect of a strategic narrative takes advantage of. It's the organisation's future told and acted out as a big story. The task at hand is to reimagine your entire strategic hierarchy as a story with a classic narrative structure. This is the story that will move employees, customers, users and collaborators to want to realise your strategy. And it's the choices you make and the actions you perform in the name of your brand that drive the story forward. When these big stories reach and engage a lot of people, that's when the brands of these stories become really strong.

We have seen how great leaders turn big stories into effective tools to help turn visions and goals into concrete action and results. The story told by John F. Kennedy in 1961(JKF Library 2016) was more like a tall tale: "I believe that this nation should commit itself to achieving the goal, before this decade is out, of landing a man on the moon and returning him safely to the earth."

A tall tale is what it would have ended up as hadn't the story been backed up by the necessary investment and willingness to take great risks to realise it. The announcement was followed by a plethora of initiatives and actions. Milestones were set and reached along the way. Over the years people were gradually more and more involved in the progress of the space programme. And then Armstrong took that first step on the moon, mesmerising a global audience more than ready for the story's climax.

Stories win over facts

To understand why stories always win over facts, let's return to the brain for a moment (Wyer 1988). When people are presented with facts, the language centres of their brains are active. When people are listening to stories however, the areas of their brains activated by experiences also light up. When we listen to stories about danger, our bodies release the stress hormone cortisol to keep the brain alert. When stories end well, the brain is rewarded with a spray of oxytocin and we feel good body and soul. Stories leave marks, plain and simple. I think most of us know what it feels like to be exhausted by a really good thriller. Or have allowed a tear to fall at the closing scene of *Love Actually*.

Neuro-economist Paul Zak (2015) has conducted several studies that show how our brains react to stories and the implications of these reactions on people's financial dispositions. In one of his experiments, people were asked to donate money to a cause after having been exposed to either a factual or an emotional story. The boring story had no effect on people's willingness to donate whatsoever. On the other hand, the story that triggered the release of empathy hormones influenced people's attitudes as well as their behaviours.

Some stories hit us harder

Looking at the great stories, the ones people have told, written and performed for each other over the millennia, we see that there are similarities between them. These stories tend to treat themes that are central to the human experience in general: the expectations of others, facing challenges, pursuing dreams and making or breaking relationships.

A story can usually be categorized as such and such kind of story quite easily, depending on the extent to which it conforms to certain story structure expectations; conventions established through our recognition of a finite number of possible plot structures. Organisations that have set their goals and defined some strategies for the journey to reach them can benefit from telling the story of this journey as a variation of one of these basic plots. The advantage being that people are already familiar with the story structure and will be able to follow your story with little effort, whether they are your employees, customers, owners or just people on the street.

One such story we all know the contours of is the story about the little guy against a greater power, the David against Goliath. Is this perhaps why people respond positively to brands that challenge large established brands outright? Look at how the Danish Noma, Norwegian Maaemo and Spanish El Bulli in its time challenged the conventions of elegant, fine dining. These cutting edge restaurant brands get far more attention from people than seems warranted when you consider the category they're in, how much they spend on marketing or how important they are to people's everyday lives. But they move us somehow, and make us pay attention to how the brands' stories progress and perhaps even compel us to take part in forwarding them.

Three assumptions

The value of having a strategic narrative, and the way I prefer working with them, are based on the following three assumptions.

1. **Managers manage more effectively when they invite and involve people in the realisation of a big story.**

   When executives talk about strategy development and implementation they tend to do so referring to facts. And even if most managers know full well that few of their staff are giddy with the anticipation of reaching EBITDA of 6.5 per cent, even objectives like increased market share, improved customer satisfaction scores or sales targets for the next quarter can fail to inspire. And these are things managers do talk about – a lot. The value of – and leaders' abilities in – storytelling in business and branding is best described in the 2007 Harvard Business review article "The four truths of the storyteller". In this article, Peter Guber explains how leaders can motivate and mobilise people by telling stories about the company that are both true and compelling.

2. **There's a difference between telling a story and living it.**
   This assumption stems from Ty Montague (2013) and his metastory concept. Montague defines metastory as a story told through action. A metastory is not a story to be told as a narrative in the traditional sense, it's the story about your brand that people understand when presented with a series of concrete actions placed in context.

3. **There's a finite set of basic plots.**
   Versions of these basic plots have been told and retold and are still being told around bonfires, as fairy tales, in books, in films and in TV series and so on. These are stories that capture us, and that shape us, because they speak of fundamental values, dilemma and conflicts that are part of growing up, finding ourselves and our place in society. In his book *The Seven Basic Plots* (2004) Christopher Booker defines such a set of basic plots and these are the set used in this book. The strategic narrative will serve its purpose better if organised – at least roughly – according to one of the basic plot structures, utilising a dramaturgy that's already recognisable to most people. In an organisation where people are made to understand that the changes necessary take on the plot structure of a rebirth, they will know to expect changes that are profound and perhaps painful, but that the objective is to emerge from them a new and reinvigorated version of itself. Perhaps this can make it easier to understand the process as they are going through it, and perhaps even push through it faster and with more positive energy.

In a sense, the strategic narrative tool has found its shape as a kind of remix of Guber's "The four truths of the storyteller" article, Montague's *True story* book and Booker's seven basic plots.

I always believed that in order to make a really great animated film, you needed to do three things: tell a compelling story that keeps people on the edge of their seat, populate that story with really memorable and appealing characters, and put that compelling story and these memorable characters in a believable world. If you can do those three things really well, then the audience will be swept away and totally entertained.

John Lasseter, 2015

Chief Creative office, Pixar and Walt Disney Animations Studios

In many ways, the structure of the models used for this tool aligns with Montague's prescribed metastory method. However, there are two reasons in particular for choosing to refer to the tool as a strategic narrative. Firstly, in my experience the terms used by Montague – metastory and storydoing – tend to feel made up and do not resonate well with the everyday language of clients. Secondly – and much more importantly – the purpose of this tool is to bring the entire organisation and other stakeholders on board in realising its strategy. So, while actor may not seem like a good metaphor to apply to people going about their day to day business, the parallel is not as silly as it seems, which makes the term narrative appropriate as well, as long as it's one that can be acted out. To play one's part in realising the strategy it's useful to know which role to play and how the things one is doing helps propel the story forward towards its ultimate goal. The strategic hierarchy will be a good support in and of itself, but it does not have the mobilising power of a great story.

The building blocks of a good story

The question of the necessary elements of good storytelling has been a bone of contention since, at least, the time of Aristotle. Nevertheless, there are a few building blocks we can usually agree are important. There's the story itself, starting with some sort of "once upon a time", and the elements that when put together make up the story.

The elements are, essentially, character, a protagonist and other central figures of the story, the environment in which the story plays out, and the events or circumstances that drive the plot forward and keep us interested as the story unfolds. We might list them like this: Red Riding Hood, grandma and the wolf, the woods, Little Red Riding Hood walks through the woods bringing food to her grandmother.

The expert storytellers at the American film studio Pixar have shared some of their storytelling wisdom in describing story structure as follows: Once upon a time there was… Every day… One day… Because of that… Because of that… Until finally. So: Once upon a time there was a girl called Little Red Riding Hood. Every day she was helpful, sweet and trusting. One day she set off to visit her grandmother's house in the woods. Because of that she ran into the wolf and revealed her errand. Because of that the wolf ate grandma and was able to trick Little Red Riding Hood and gobble her up too. Until finally the hunter showed up, slayed the wolf and rescued grandma and Little Red Riding Hood from its belly.

As the example above illustrates well – just knowing how the story goes is not enough to make it exciting. It's only when the scenes are expanded with colourful detail that the elements put together can evolve into an immortal tale. The characters' motives must be possible to grasp, and events perceived as happening in some sort of causal context. This is what businesses and organisation need to work on to make sure employees and customers alike understand and want to participate in their story.

The story elements
The main character – or protagonist
The main character is the brand. What can be said about the organisation, what it offers, or the business and the state it's in? Which role does the brand play in its market? What does your organisation care about? What are your people doing and what are they talking about? What are your brand's real strengths and what makes it weak or exposed? What was the start of your business, and where is it headed? Which are some of your organisation's longest standing values and which are particularly strong and relevant today?

The rest of the cast
The other participants in your story are all the people touched by your brand, whether customers or users, owners with a clear agenda of their own or anyone else who is affected by what the protagonist chooses to do. What are their motivations? What role does the protagonist play in their lives? How can the protagonist's story improve their lives or the stories they tell about themselves? Do any of these characters resist or seek to undermine the protagonist's project or the values of your brand?

The stage
This is the environment in which the story unfolds. What characterises the cultural, technological, economic or demographic scene of your story? Is something significant afoot? Is the competitive arena fuzzy or clear? Does the protagonist have enemies, or are there forces at play that represent a threat to your existence, or quite the opposite? Can you spot emerging trends that work in your favour, or that make it trickier for your brand to succeed, that play to your brand's particular strengths or weaknesses?

The quest
The last story element, perhaps the most important one, is the protagonist's quest. What is it the protagonist wants to do for customers, its community, the organisation it belongs to or the world as such? What is the task at hand or the quest that can be the stated mission of your organisation, or a higher ideal, speaking to a particular lifestyle or the values that your product or services promote? A quest can be perpetual, such as Red Bull's quest to give people wings or the American fast food chain Chipotle's ambition to cultivate a better world. Or it can be specific to a point in time, or to a particular opportunity sought, or tied to a threat such as a technological shift or climate change.

> It's unlikely that any one person has the whole picture. But when it's all put together, there is truth there to be discovered; a truth that can be shared by everyone.

Pinning down the story elements

Most of the work to fill the story elements with content has already been done through your work with the brand platform and the strategic hierarchy. You'll have a lot of insights from your study of your brand's competitive arena, from the differentiation process, understanding your customers' motivations and your own brand identity. Put everything you think might be relevant up on a wall, and study it with the eye of a storyteller. When describing your protagonist, your brand's role in its category will be particularly important. As will the relationship between the brand and its customers. When looking at the wider cast of your story, you might want to zoom in on the identity prism, particularly the parts that deal with your customers' reflection and self-image. Your category and the competitive arena is a good place to start when you want to describe the stage or the environment of your story. And as for the quest, the most obvious starting point from which to develop a compelling story about your brand is your mission and values statement.

If you feel like there's still something missing after you're done defining your story elements, and that you don't really have the necessary building blocks to craft your story, now is the time to supplement. It may be that insights or elements that didn't seem that important early on in your branding process, should be revisited and perhaps given a more prominent place in your story.

Here's a checklist you can use if you're looking to give the story elements a thorough shake:
1. Live your customers' life. What does the world and the protagonist look like from their perspective?
2. Seek outside-in information. Talk to experts in your field, customers, competitors and previous employees if they're up for it.
3. Interview people in confidence. What do they *really* think about your business/organisation? What do they think of your competitors and what's their perspective on possible substitutes or intruders in the competitive arena? Understand how the size of your business, your company culture, your operations, or your financial situation affects people's perceptions. How do people define success and where do they see you in three to five years?
4. Perform an honest and thorough review of your brand/company as well as any relevant rivals/substitutes. Find information about your founders; learn about the history of your business, what was the original ambition and how did that lead to your current products or services?
5. How do people feel about the times they live in? Is there something going on that's likely to influence the competitive landscape? Will emerging trends, technological, economic or demographic conditions shift established positions in your category?
6. Make sure you understand the management position by talking to the organisation's leaders and other key figures. What motivates them? Which competitors do they particularly enjoy taking business from?
7. Calibrate the information. It's unlikely that any one person has the whole picture. But when it's all put together, there is truth there to be discovered; a truth that can be shared by everyone.

The starting point of a strategic narrative

Before moving on to what in *True Story* is called a metastory, or the story told by the organisation through its actions, it's worth taking a little detour outside Montague's framework. We take this detour for a couple of reasons. Firstly, it's a rare thing for a business leader or organisation management teams to also be script-writing virtuosos. Unfortunately, the stories they define tend to be somewhat less engaging to other people. The second is that this particular kind of story unfolds over time. Think of it as a one-thousand-day-story simply because the realisation of an ambitious strategy will take time. The strategy must be told, understood, internalised and lived, acted out bit by bit through people's choices and actions. This again must be perceived by the outside world and spread until it becomes a true story, recognised internally as well as externally. This means that your story needs to have the power to engage and maintain people's interest over the course of years.

> **Your story needs to have the power to engage and maintain people's interest over the course of years.**

To guide us in this work, I have found *The Seven Basic Plots: Why we tell stories* (2004) by Christopher Booker immensely useful. Booker's claim is that all the stories in the world are founded in themes that are common to the human experience and therefore told over and over again in new variations of the same basic plots. Booker is not the only one to make this point, and other scholars with similar projects may reach a different number of plot structures, but for our purpose, how many plots there *really* are is not the interesting question. So, we'll leave that particular issue to others. However, Booker's seven plot structures is a highly fit for purpose framework for people looking to translate a company strategy into a compelling story.

Below you will find summaries of the seven basic plots. I have tried to describe them faithfully even if these are brutally abridged interpretations. I have also aimed to describe what kind of situations or circumstances make each of the plot structures appropriate as a starting point for your brand's strategic narrative. Each organisation will naturally have its own unique opportunities. Leaders and management teams will have varying ambitions and preferences, which is also absolutely fine.

Overcoming the monster

This kind of story begins in ordinary times where people live happily ignorant of a great threat looming. Whether the threat comes in the form of moral decay, a meteorite falling towards earth or an approaching enemy army, life can't go on like it used to once the danger has been discovered. The hero, or heroes, must confront the monster, taking it upon themselves to fight the good fight on behalf of the threatened community. Against terrifying odds and at great danger to the hero, the monster is slain or driven off and the people are liberated. Civilization can return to its normal happy state.

If a company or an organisation would like to structure its strategic narrative in line with this basic plot, two necessary conditions apply. Firstly, there needs to be a real threat present. The threat must be recognised and considered meaningful by your customers or most people, whether the threat is local or global. Secondly, the company or organisation's commitment to confronting and overcoming the threat must be equally real and it must have and commit the resources to do so. Tesla's story can be interpreted as a version of overcoming the monster. When the rest of the auto industry stand passively by and watch the threat of climate change grow more menacing day by day, Elon Musk with his Tesla takes it upon himself to demonstrate to the world that electricity is the future.

The quest

The protagonist hears a call and accepts an important mission. To solve the mission, he must venture into a strange, perhaps secret, world. The story moves forward towards the resolution of the quest through a series of setbacks in the form of different kinds of trouble, resistance and complications. At the same time, an enemy, or some sort of threat to society, move in on the protagonist or the protagonist's community. The main character will eventually reach his or her quest through a combination of skill, good values and a group of helpers that appear just as they are needed the most. Frodo the hobbit with his pure heart and loyal group of friends is the only one who can carry the ring to Mordor to destroy it.

The quest can be a good narrative structure for entrepreneurs: "We will take on the…industry and give the world…" Like Uber wanting to give everybody a private driver, or Microsoft who dreamt of a world where every home had a personal computer. This basic plot can work well for pioneer brands that challenge an entire industry's way of thinking, or for entrepreneurs entering new markets where established brands will fight to protect their positions. Helpers, whether distributors, brand advocates or customers and social media followers, have important supporting actor parts to play. When the entrepreneur wins, defeating the established giants, everybody wins.

However, this is also a plot structure that can serve well established brands, provided that there is a quest for them and that they mean business in accepting the call to solve it. I have always liked IKEA's "A better everyday life for the many people", which can easily be written as a quest script.

Rags to riches

The American dream long preceded the United States of America, of course. Stories about young men or women that appear as if from nowhere to conquer the world come in many shapes and forms and are common across times and cultures.

The world of sports is ripe with legends of ordinary people who by talent, perseverance and a winning personality go from obscurity to world fame. Who hasn't teared up in some dark cinema watching stories like *Pretty Woman*, *Rocky*, *Moneyball* or similar tearjerkers unfold?

This story line may appear attractive for entrepreneurs or brands that plan to expand from a niche audience to a much wider target group. However, for the story to serve its purpose, it must appeal and engage in general, not just to the entrepreneurs themselves. In my opinion, the brands that exploit this narrative most successfully tend to be those that have a colourful or surprising origin. In combination with other genre appropriate elements and lucky breaks, this origin myth can be a good springboard for a tale of continued development and growth.

3M's Post-it notes – described as the solution to a problem nobody knew existed – came about through a failed attempt at creating a super strong adhesive (CNN 2017). However, the 3M scientist working on it saw potential in the failure, and thought there might be some utility in the not very strong but re-usable and pressure sensitive adhesive. It took years of promoting the concept to 3M executives before he was allowed to create a commercial product. When he was finally able to do so, initial results were disappointing, but 3M persevered and we all know how the story went.

Storytelling is by far the most underrated skill in business

Gary Vaynerchuk

CRUSH IT!: Why NOW Is the Time to Cash In on Your Passion, 2009

Consider also the origin of Airbnb. The brand tells a story of origin by accident, where a scheme to make a little money by offering sleepovers on their air mattress, gave the young entrepreneurs their idea for a global brand and a movement to create *one less stranger* sleepover by sleepover.

Richard Branson, with his dyslexia and struggle to get through school, who went on to create the Virgin phenomenon is also a good example of a rags to riches storyline.

Rebirth

This story structure may be my personal favourite. Perhaps because it's the plot that's most demanding to realise, but if done properly has within it enormous potential for rewards.

At the start of a rebirth story, the main character is lost, perhaps oppressed, selfish or morally out of whack. At the point where things just can't get any worse, there is a transformative event. Something happens to make our hero see the light and turn against/kill/destroy the negative forces. Through gradually readjusting to a normal existence the main character is able, once again to successfully earn the respect and love of his or her fellows.

An extraordinary degree of insight, courage and leadership is required for an organisation to work its way through a story of rebirth. One of the clearest benefits of doing so is the separation of what was *then* from what is *now*. If an organisation is able to successfully persuade customers users and/or society at large that a true transformation has taken place, it can also successfully leave the old brand identity behind with all the benefits that entails. Look at how Netflix transformed itself in the effort to remain relevant in the movie distribution category. It's easy to say today that the transition from the distribution of physical film formats like DVD by post to the on demand streaming services was a necessary one, but it was probably quite painful for the organisation at the time.

Domino's Pizza went through a dramatic and public rebirth. There was a time when the business had rationalised astray and efficiency had replaced the love of food. Reviews were brutal. Domino's decided to use this low point as a rock bottom from

Marketing is no longer about the stuff you make, but about the stories you tell.

Seth Godin

All Marketers Are Liars, 2005

which to kick its way back up by reinventing itself from crust, to sauce to cheese and all the way back to the love of pizza. As a proof that it's possible to bounce back, stock prices have kept rising since the turnaround and the business has never looked back.

If, however, only pockets of the organisation are willing to transform while the rest carry on business as usual, this strategic narrative can only make matters worse. If the renewal is not seen as genuine and profound, but rather as shallow and only for show, the brand's relationship with its customers is more likely to deteriorate than to heal.

Voyage and return

Whether it's Alice's adventures in Wonderland, Nemo who abandons the safety of his coral reef or Marty McFly stuck in the past finding his way back to the future, the voyage and return plot line is most of all about discovering resources within the main character through the exploration of a strange world. Most of us can recognise the experience of growing as people (or almost losing ourselves) as a result of getting to know or becoming part of new groups and environments. This plot structure is common to stories about self-realisation and coming of age.

This is also an angle much loved by the popular media. Stories tend to be captivating and easy to tell as well as follow ("The disease made me stronger", "Transformed by love"). Politicians, activists and aid organisations of many shapes and forms apply this structure to their storytelling, often by bringing leaders, celebrities and other ambassadors to environments that demonstrate aspects of their cause and reporting on how that person was transformed somehow by the experience.

The difference between this story structure and for example the quest or overcoming the monster is that a voyage and return story finds its forward momentum in the exploration of the new environment itself, rather than towards a particular goal or to avert a defined threat to society. It's a story line that can work well for brands that are well established in their primary markets, but are looking to explore new target groups, other categories or expand to new markets without alienating existing customer groups. This plot structure provides the liberty to frame the new initiatives as explorations, where a return home is not a failure, but rather the conclusion of a learning experience. Such a strategic narrative can be an invitation for people to join in, to help, support and explore the new opportunities together with the brand to see if there are things to learn or fun to be had together.

It's also possible to see Pret A Manger's journey into McDonald's land and back again as a voyage and return story. The first Pret A Manger shop was opened in London in the 1980s and was a pioneer in the fresh, natural, fast food category. In the early 2000s, McDonald bought about a third of the company. While the move took a lot of people by surprise – this was a match people didn't really see coming – it did help fund Pret's expansion of the chain beyond the UK. A few years later, McDonald's divested its share of the company, but by then Pret A Manger had grown to a global brand, stronger and wiser (Marketing Week 2017).

There aren't too many examples of brands that choose to live by this narrative despite the opportunities it offers. Perhaps we are afraid people will perceive this type of exploration strategy as frivolous or inconsistent? Either way, some newer brands that are built on strong relationships with their customers or users are living this story line in launching new initiatives, gauging people's interest, adjusting accordingly and just making sure to keep friends and acquaintances informed and included along the ride.

Look at Google with its "moonshots" and other experimental services that may or may not be viable. There's no failure in trying different things out.

Comedy

A comedy is light and entertaining and has likeable characters and a happy ending. However, comedy is not all laughter and gags, it's also a story structure that has finding a way out of confusing circumstances at its core. In a comedic story structure, there will typically be some sort of event to kick off the story. After this first event, it's the main character itself, the other participants in the story, and the environment in which the story unfolds that introduce confusion and complication to the point where it's hard to even understand what's going on. In the end, the complications all untangle and confusion is resolved.

This basic plot should only provide structure to the strategic narrative of brands with considerable goodwill, and that have brand identities that lend themselves to comedy. In our day and age, the most popular comedies are romantic, so this could be a good script structure for brands that want to be loved themselves or that are all about bringing people closer together.

Tragedy

The tragic plot structure follows the trajectory of a main character that meets an untimely end mainly due to a grave mistake or as a result of a flawed character. Never mind the pity potential inherent in such a plot structure, no brand will want this particular story line as the back bone of its strategic narrative.

Inadvertently, companies and brands have stumbled into it and reached great fame as people have followed their fall: Enron with its corrupt management, Kodak for failing to see what lay ahead, and the Lehman Brothers sinking under the weight of rotten loans during the 2008 financial crisis.

If you feel that this tragic story structure may be a bit too close to home, make a speedy switch to Rebirth. It's never too late to try a better path.

Which story is the right story?

Well, first of all, the story structure must be possible for the brand, so round one is to simply eliminate the ones that just don't work. If your brand is well established and well known, rags to riches will probably not be the one for you, unless you're bringing your brand to a new category, target group or new geographic area. If there's no real threat that your brand can play an important part in warding off, well then overcoming the monster will not be available to your strategic narrative. And so on.

Once you are left with a couple of possible alternatives, it's a good idea to simply write them and see how they might work as a structure for your strategic narrative. Write the story as if writing it from a future where the story has ended in the best possible way. Make use of the basic plot elements and fill in the content of your strategy to take your brand from where it is now to where it is going. You'll discover that the story changes depending on whether you align it with a quest-plot or a rebirth. As you tell the story, what becomes clearer with regard to the competitive arena? Or the relationship between the brand and its users? Is the story being told a story that engages the organisation or its owners, or does the story line follow a dramaturgy that the market, customers in particular, will follow with interest over time? Will they want to play a part in it? Will the people who work for the brand be energized and understand what to do to move the story forward? Which of the story structures provides the best framework for conveying the nature and speed of changes that lie ahead?

In my own experience of preparing alternative script suggestions for client workshops and the like, it's sometimes unclear to me exactly which story structure has the best fit for the brand's journey. But when leaders and management groups review my suggestions, there's seldom any doubt – they tend to zoom unanimously in on one of the alternatives as the right one. And as before, while it's a good idea to qualify first impressions, stories do trump facts. If it feels right, it may just be right.

Nine things brand builders do well to remember

If you've read this far, you know a lot already. Perhaps you have already had an opportunity to test some of the tools in practice, or discuss them with colleagues? Either way, here's nine pieces of advice based on what I've learned from working with this framework over the years – as a thank you from me to you for bearing with me through this book.

1 Be visionary, but know reality.

The biggest mistake you can make is to build your brand taking its strengths as your starting point. Just don't. Understand the competitive arena from your customers' perspective and by studying the positions taken by other brands. Find a position that's relevant, credible, differentiated and realistic. Then go for it.

2 Be something.

Category is the door to people's minds. If you do nothing else for your brand, at least make sure you know what category it's in or wants to build. If you're establishing a new category or breaking up an existing one into smaller sub categories, start from something familiar and give it an exciting and relevant twist.

3 Take your role seriously.

If the brand is a market leader, the brand should take responsibility for developing the category for everyone. If the brand is a challenger, it should accept the market leader's power of definition and stand out as a clear alternative to it. If the brand is or wants to become a pioneer, be very clear about what it is bringing to the table that's new or how it plans to transform its industry.

4 Learn the rules, then decide how to play the game.
Differentiation is all about understanding what criteria are important to customers' decisions, and then deciding a unique way for your brand to fulfil those criteria. The more criteria you take a systematic position on, the harder it will be for others to copy. Anyone can copy a single measure, but a whole pattern of strategic choices is harder to adopt.

5 Be unique.
Be strategic, but also authentic, and consistent most of all. Strong brands stand out like iconic personalities – unique and compelling. Once you have decided what your brand should be in people's minds, take every opportunity to reinforce that impression, throughout your business, in every touch point, in all communication, all the time. Remember that even the strongest brands have access to only the tiniest bandwidth of our brains, so work relentlessly to leave the same impression every time. Always.

6 Know yourself.
Understand people's motivation for choosing your brand above others. Respond to these motivations through an archetypical identity. We all recognise the archetypes intuitively. You will discover how much energy and creativity is unleashed when you set your organisation and culture free to channel that identity in everything they do.

7 Build your identity with relationships in mind.

Brands are built in the intersecting field of your organisation, its customers and the products and services offered. Always put this relationship first and never, ever be tempted to build the brand from your own perspective.

8 Strategy includes brand strategy.

You can make as many strategies as you want, benchmark away, map customer journeys, discover new business models all day long and involve everybody if you like. It will do you very little good, unless you remember to also build something in people's minds. If your brand can find a place in people's minds – and hearts – you can always adapt, adjust, and develop the rest, finding ways to create exciting things together with your customers.

9 Create your (hi)story!

Everybody likes a good story, and we all want to be a part of one. When management knows where it's going with a brand and has decided how to get there, start living the journey as a story together. Make sure to include people, cheer them on as they sign up, and mobilise participation in events large and small that show exactly where this story is headed.

Thanks for your company

From blueprint to realisation

A good start

For those of you that have worked your way through positioning and identity, you now have a broad blueprint to work from. As a result, your brand is less dependent on individual brand authorities taking intuitive brand development decisions, whether those persons might be the founders, a leader or product development director, marketing or communications person.

If your brand platform has been integrated with how the overall business strategy is communicated, and you have worked out a clear description of what your organisation aims to achieve over the next years, you have a good foundation from which to engage and mobilise your people.

It's the entire organisation's job to nurture the brand's relationship with its customers and other stakeholders. That's also the brand's most important job. The brand identity can develop in time with its role, its mission and trends just like people can, but it must nevertheless stay true to its fundamental values and its history. It's easier to maintain your brand's relevance as it grows in and out of different roles and categories if the entire organisation is in a position to strengthen the brand as a part of their day to day operations. That's when a brand has become a fully integrated part of the organisation's strategy.

A blueprint, however, is not the same thing as a fully realised product. Nor is a skilled and dedicated organisation with detailed instruction about where it's going sufficient to ensure the realisation of a shared vision. When it comes to building strong brands a *what* and a *why* without the *how* is about as clear as mud. Similarly, a *how* without a *what* and *why* is just a series of rote tasks. We have to understand all of these. Even so, strategy development and strategy implementation is not quite the same thing. In this book, I write primarily about the former.

I end this book where it started, with a wish that you, dear reader, have found something here that might help you dig a little deeper so that you may aim even higher on behalf of the brands you're working with. I hope also, that you may see greater potential in using the power of the brand to unleash the positive forces necessary to develop your business to its fullest potential, regardless of whether you work with or for the brand in the capacity of management, communications, consultant or student.

For business leaders with no marketing background, I hope the book has provided some new insights that you want to start making use of.

For marketers, I hope this book has motivated you to develop solid and strong brand platforms, and that you've been able to use it as a guide in your day to day job and perhaps inspired you to keep fighting for the importance of brand strategy in your organisation or business.

If you're an advisor or consultant, I hope I've provided you with some new tools and the motivation to seek out other tools for the areas not covered extensively in the book, such as successful strategy implementation.

For designers and other creative forces, it is my wish that this book might encourage you to use well founded brand platforms as spring boards and see where it takes you when you apply your creative genius.

For students, it is my particular wish that this book might motivate you to study and make use of the emerging academic research in our field, so that you can build the new strong brands for our future. That's never been more important than it is right now.

A real threat and a golden opportunity

As a result of the digital shift we are experiencing, local brands in industry after industry are facing global competition to an extent never seen before. Amazon is undermining the traditional business models of the publishing world, Facebook is disrupting the distribution of news and Uber is messing with the conventions of human transportation pretty much everywhere.

We are also in the middle of a sustainability shift. The global community, its international institutions, global initiatives, government regulations, business innovations and individual actions must build a more sustainable future. As the awareness of the challenges ahead as well as the opportunities they offer grow, sustainable practices and aspirations are being built into strategies and brand platforms alike. Opportunities will be seized by early movers and late adapters will suffer. GE's mission "to invent the next industrial era, to build, move, power and cure the world" being a case in point.

So as you can see, there are a few good reasons to be optimistic on behalf of the brands of the future, even in this era of global megabrands. The first reason is that just like we are open to accepting global brands, the world is also open to accepting local brands that have the skills as well as courage to position themselves in the International arena. However, this depends on being just as skilled in positioning brands clearly in people's minds as in building competitive products and services.

The second reason to be optimistic is the shift from the old kind of branding built on a promise, to the new kind built on a bond or meaningful relationship. Emerging organisations and innovative businesses tend to have flatter structures, less micro management and a high degree of trust/responsibility. This is exactly the kind of environment that encourages people to take responsibility for and make independent choices that strengthen the customer relationship, across any organisational silos or decision-making hierarchies.

Who knows what the limits are and which innovations we'll see in the years to come. What we can expect, however, is that what ever next big thing is coming, we'll get to know it as a clearly defined and understood brand as well as a product or service. The competition for love, attention and a market share of people's minds is at least as important as the competition for market share on the ground. Wouldn't you like to discover just how far you can take the *real* potential of your brand?

List of references

Aaker, David A. (1992). *Managing Brand Equity*. New York: The Free Press.

Aaker, David and Joachimstaler, Erick. (2000). *Brand Leadership*. New York: The Free Press.

Absolut (27.08.2016). www.theabsolutcompany.com

Absolut Vodka. (28.08.2016). http://www.theabsolutcompany.com/absolut-vodka/

Adidas (15.08.2016). https://en.wikipedia.org/wiki/Adidas_Superstar

Airbnb (11.09.2016). http://blog.airbnb.com/who-we-are/

Amazon (30.10.2016). https://www.facebook.com/Amazon/about

Antzoulatos, Evan G. and Miller, Earl K. (2011). Differences between Neural Activity in Prefrontal Cortex and Striatum during Learning of Novel Abstract Categories, *Neuron* Cell Press.

Apple (13.08.2016). https://www.apple.com/iPhone-6s/

Apple (2001). https://www.apple.com/pr/library/2001/10/23Apple-Presents-iPod.html

Apple (2007). http://www.apple.com/pr/library/2007/01/09Apple-Reinvents-the-Phone-with-iPhone.html

Apple (2010). http://www.apple.com/pr/library/2010/01/27Apple-Launches-iPad.html

Apple (18.02.2018). https://www.apple.com/watch/

Bed Head, (15.08.2016). http://www.bedhead.com/en/#

Bitcoin (15.08.2016). https://bitcoin.org/en/

Booker Christopher (2004). *The seven basic plots: Why we tell stories*. London: Continuum.

Brewdog (15.08.2016). https://www.brewdog.com/about/history

Brown, Tim (2009). *Change by Design. How Design Thinking Transforms Organizations and Inspires Innovation*. Harper Collins.

Bughin, Jacques, Doogan, Jonathan and Vetvik, Ole Jørgen (April 2010). A new way to measure word-of-mouth marketing. *McKinsey Quarterly*.

Cern. (25.11.2017). https://home.cern/about

Cialdini, Robert (2006). *Influence. The psychology of persuasion*. Harper Business.

CNN. (28.11.2017). http://edition.cnn.com/2013/04/04/tech/post-it-note-history/index.html

Coats, Emma (2011). *Pixar's 22 rules of storytelling*. (28.11.2017). http://io9.gizmodo.com/5916970/the-22-rules-of-storytelling-according-to-pixar

Collins, Jim and Porras, Jerry I. (1996). Building your company's vision. *Harvard Business Review*. (15.08.2016). https://hbr.org/1996/09/building-your-companys-vision

Collis, David and Rukstad, Michael (2008). *Can you say what your strategy is?* https://hbr.org/2008/04/can-you-say-what-your-strategy-is

Court, David, Elzinga, Dave, Mulder, Susan, and Vetvik, Ole Jørgen (2009). The Consumer Decision Journey. *McKinsey Quarterly.*

Diesel (15.08.2016). http://store.diesel.com/magazine/en/world-of-diesel/about-diesel/

Economist. (2009). http://www.economist.com/node/13766375;

Edelman, David and Singer, Marc (2015). The New Consumer Decision Journey. *McKinsey Quarterly.*

Encyclopædia Britannica. (28.11.2017). https://www.britannica.com/topic/archetype

Encyclopædia Britannica. (28.11.2017). https://www.britannica.com/topic/role

Fastco Design (15.08.2016). http://www.fastcodesign.com/3035746/fast-feed/vivienne-westwoods-virgin-atlantic-uniforms-apparently-make-flight-attendants-blee

Financial Samurai. (15.08.2016). *The New Rule For Engagement Ring Buying.* http://www.financialsamurai.com/the-new-rule-for-engagement-ring-buying/

GE. (2014). http://www.ge.com/ar2014/ceo-letter/

Godin, Seth. 2009. All marketers are liars: the power of telling authentic stories in a low-trust world. New York: Portfolio.

Google (03.09.2016). https://www.google.com/selfdrivingcar/

Google (15.08.2016). https://www.google.com/intl/en/about/

Google (15.08.2016). https://www.google.com/intl/en/about/company/philosophy/

Guardian (2004). https://www.theguardian.com/media/2004/nov/01/marketingandpr

Guber, Peter (2007). The four truths of the storyteller. *Harvard Business Review*, 85(12):52–59, 142. https://hbr.org/2007/12/the-four-truths-of-the-storyteller/es

Hartwell, Margaret and Chen, C. Joshua (2012). *Archetypes in branding*, Ohio: HOW Books.

Havas. (15.08.2016). Havas' Meaningful Brands® 2015 study http://www.havasmedia.com/press/press-releases/2015/top-scoring-meaningful-brands-enjoy-a-share-of-wallet-46-per-cent-higher-than-low-performers

Heath, Chip and Heath, Dan (2008). Selling your innovation. Fast Company. 07.01.2008. (15.05.2018). https://www.fastcompany.com/898662/selling-your-innovation-anchor-and-twist

Heath, Chip and Heath, Dan (2011). *Switch.* New York: Random House Business Books. http://heathbrothers.com/books/switch/

Heath, Dan. (2010). *How to Write a Mission Statement That Doesn't Suck.* https://www.youtube.com/watch?v=LJhG3HZ7b4o

Holden, Mark and Devoy, Maloolm (2012). *Overthrow: Ten ways to tell a challenger story.* London, PHD Worldwide.

IBM https://www.ibm.com/developerworks/community/blogs/0fbe83eb-1b06-4f42-b5f3-45cd0a1dd129/entry/thomas_j_watson_on_developerworks16?lang=en

Innocent. 2007. (28.11.2017). http://innocentdrinks.typepad.com/innocent_drinks/our_drinks/page/9/

JFK Library. http://www.jfklibrary.org/JFK/JFK-Legacy/NASA-Moon-Landing.aspx

Johnson & Johnson (15.08.2016). http://www.jnj.com/sites/default/files/pdf/jnj_ourcredo_english_us_8.5×11_cmyk.pdf

Jones, Richard G. Jr. (2013). *Communication in the Real World: An Introduction to Communication Studies*, v. 1.0. (15.08.2016). http://catalog.flatworldknowledge.com/bookhub/reader/8027?e=jones_1.0-ch01_s02#jones_1.0-ch01_s02

Kapferer, Jean Noel (2012). *Strategic Brand Management*, rev. 5. Paris: Les Editions d'Organisation.

Kaplan, Robert S. and Norton, David P. (2004). *Strategy Maps: Converting Intangible Assets into Tangible Outcomes*. Harvard Business School Publishing.

Keller, Kevin Lane (1998). *Strategic Brand Management*, s. 308. Upper Saddle River, NJ: Prentice Hall.

Keller, Kevin Lane, Sternthal, Brian and Tybout, Alice M. (2002). Three Questions You Need to Ask About Your Brand. *Harvard Business Review* 80(9):80–86, 125. https://hbr.org/2002/09/three-questions-you-need-to-ask-about-your-brand

Keynes, John Maynard (1936). The General Theory of Employment, Interest and Money. London: Macmillan.

Kotler, Philip and Keller, Kevin Lane et al. (2015). *Marketing Management*. Upper Saddle River, New Jersey: Pearson Education.

Kotter, John P. (2012). *Leading Change*. Boston, MA: Harvard Business Review Press.

Kotter, John P. (2014). *AXL8*. Boston, MA: Harvard Business Review Press.

LA Times. (2015). http://www.latimes.com/la-fi-hy-elon-musk-big-ideas-story-so-far-20150501-htmlstory.html

Lasseter, John. 2015. Pixar: the design of story. (15.05.2018). https://collection.cooperhewitt.org/exhibitions/102147315/

Latin Dictionary. (16.05.2018). http://latindictionary.wikidot.com/verb:valere

Lego. (30.10.2016). https://wwwsecure.lego.com/en-us/aboutus/lego-group/mission-and-vision

Levitt, Theodore (1986). *The marketing imagination* (New expanded ed.). New York: The Free Press.

Lewis, E. St. Elmo (1903). Catch-Line and Argument. *The Book-Keeper*, vol. 15, s. 124.

Lloyds Register. (15.08.2016). http://www.careers.lr.org/about-us/our-mission

Macworld. (15.08.2016). Steve Jobs http://www.macworld.co.uk/feature/apple/history-of-apple-steve-jobs-what-happened-mac-computer-3606104/#1984

Maaemo. (27.08.2016). (www.maaemo.no)

Mark, Margaret and Pearson, Carol (2001). *The Hero and the Outlaw*. New York: McGraw-Hill.

Marketing Week. *(28.11.2017)*. https://www.marketingweek.com/2009/01/01/pret-a-manger-aims-to-dispel-mcdonalds-myth/

McCarthy, E. Jerome (1960). *Basic Marketing. A Managerial Approach*. Homewood, IL: Richard D. Irwin.

Millward Brown (2012). *Brandz Top 100 Global Brands Report 2012*. New York: Millward Brown.

Monarth, Harrison (2014). The irresistible power of storytelling as a strategic business tool. *Harvard Business Review*, 11. March 2014. (15.08.2016). https://hbr.org/2014/03/the-irresistible-power-of-storytelling-as-a-strategic-business-tool

Montague, Ty (2013). *True Story*. Boston: Harvard Business School Publishing.

Morgan, Adam and Holden, Mark. (2009). *Eating the big fish*. Hoboken, New Jersey: John Wiley & Sons Inc.

New York Times. (2002). http://www.nytimes.com/2002/01/19/opinion/enron-s-vision-and-values-thing.html

New York Times. *(28.11.2017)*. https://www.nytimes.com/2017/04/05/business/kendall-jenner-pepsi-ad.html?_r=0, 2017

Nike. (15.08.2016). us.nike.com/app/answers/detail/a_id/113/~/nike-mission-statement

Nike. (15.08.2016). http://news.nike.com/news/nike-launches-find-your-greatness-campaign-celebrating-inspiration-for-the-everyday-athlete

Osterwalder, Alexander and Pigneur, Yves (2010). *Business Model Generation: A Handbook for Visionaries, Game Changers, and Challengers*. Hoboken: John Wiley & Sons.

Oxford Dictionaries. (15.08.2016). http://www.oxforddictionaries.com/definition/english/value

Porter, Michael E. (1996). What is strategy? *Harvard Business Review* 74(6):61–78.

Procter & Gamble. (2012). Best Job. https://www.youtube.com/watch?v=HO5O_FZfwXs&index=14&list=PLLIVyCflGKKd8T7iX4pi0t0nuMpQcEWas

Prophet, *Brand Relevance Index*. *(28.11.2017)*. https://www.prophet.com/relevantbrands-2016/uk.pdf

Prophet. *(28.11.2017)*. https://www.prophet.com/thinking/2014/02/5-lessons-from-t-mobiles-game-changing-strategy/)

Quora. (13.08.2016). https://www.quora.com/Did-Peter-Drucker-actually-say-culture-eats-strategy-for-breakfast-and-if-so-where-when

Ridgway, Steve (2011). How we see it – Three senior executives on the future of marketing. *McKinsey Quarterly*.

Ries, Al and Ries, Laura (2002). *22 Immutable laws of branding*. Harper Business.

Ries, Al and Trout, Jack (1994). *22 immutable laws of marketing*. Harper Collins.

SiS. (15.05.2018). Product information. https://www.scienceinsport.com/us/sis-rego-rapid-recovery-protein-500g-chocolate-usa-c4885e3bdde25bb09252c6f3a8f74827

SiS. (15.05.2018). Press release. https://www.snewsnet.com/press-release/science-in-sport-now-fueling-three-of-the-worlds-strongest-cycling-organizations

Steen Van den, Eric. Strategy and Strategic Decisions. *Harvard Business School Technical Note 712–500, June 2012.*

Storydoing. (15.08.2016). www.storydoing.com

Telenor https://www.telenor.com/no/om-oss/visjon-og-verdier/

Thompson, Arthur, Peteraf, Margaret, Gamble, John and Strickland III, A.J. (2012). *Crafting & Executing Strategy.* New York: McGraw Hill.

Toms. (15.08.2016). http://www.toms.com/improving-lives

Under Armour. *(28.11.2017).* https://en.wikipedia.org/wiki/Under_Armour

Unilever. (10.02.2018). https://www.unilever.com/news/news-and-features/Feature-article/2017/is-it-ok-for-guys-axe-says-yes.html

Vaynerchuk, Gary. 2009. Crush It!: Why NOW Is the Time to Cash In on Your Passion. New York: HarperStudio.

Wikileaks. (15.08.2016). https://wikileaks.org/What-is-Wikileaks.html

Wikipedia. (20.08.2016). https://en.wikipedia.org/wiki/Abraham_Maslow

Wikipedia. (20.08.2016). https://en.wikipedia.org/wiki/Big_Hairy_Audacious_GoalStore

Wikipedia. (20.08.2016). https://en.wikipedia.org/wiki/General_Electric

Wikipedia. (20.08.2016). https://en.wikipedia.org/wiki/John_Kotter

Wikipedia. (20.08.2016). https://en.wikipedia.org/wiki/Points-of-parity/points-of-difference

Wikipedia. (20.08.2016). https://en.wikipedia.org/wiki/Storytelling

Wikipedia. (20.08.2016). https://en.wikipedia.org/wiki/Think_(IBM)

Wikipedia. (20.08.2016). https://en.wikipedia.org/wiki/Think_different

Wikipedia. (20.08.2016). https://en.wikipedia.org/wiki/Vision_statement

Wikipedia. (20.11.2017). https://en.wikipedia.org/wiki/Jack_Daniel%27s

Wyer, Robert S. Jr. (1988). Advances in Social Cognition, volume 8, Erlbaum.

Zak, Paul J. (2015). Why inspiring stories make us react: The neuroscience of narrative? *Cerebrum: 10.*

Keyword list

A

Advocate 28
AIDA 33
Anchor and twist 61
Archetypes 110, 113
Associations 29

B

Basic plots 243
Basic Plots 250
BCG-matrixes 34
Behaviour 31
Big Hairy Audacious Goal 232
Big opportunity 204
Bond 114
Brain 49, 240
Brand 29, 33
Brand building 37
Brand communication 180
Brand equity model 34
Brand experiences 27
Brand identity 109, 188
Brand Identity Planning Model 34
Brand Key 34
Brand personality 41
Brand platform 41, 193, 210
Brand positioning 40
Brand promises 29
Brand's identity 41
Brand strategy 20
Business idea 212
Business Model Canvas 207
Business Model Generation 34
Business strategy 20, 84, 99, 202, 210, 227

C

Categorisation 50
Category 49
Category ambassador 70
Category attribute 58
Category criteria 91
Category rules 57
Category traits 53
Challenger 65, 66, 72
Challenger scripts 75, 97
Change 205
Change management 203
Comedy 269
Communication models 181
Competitive advantages 84
Competitive arena 28, 56, 85
Context 181
Corporate social responsibility 90
Creation myth 188
Creator 121
Culture 42, 100, 188, 194, 198, 214
Customer decision journey 35
Customer experience 27, 39
Customer journey 35

D

Decentralised decision-making 196
Decision journey 39
Design Thinking 34
Differentiating criteria 93
Differentiation 61, 83
Differentiation criteria 87
Distribution power 28, 74
Dramatic composition 239
Dramaturgy 272
Dynamic strategy 39

E

Emotional 37
Emotional and functional criteria 37
Emotional relationship 31
Establish a new category 52
Explorer 121

F

Fast follower 56
First mover 56
Functional 37
Fundamental beliefs 214

G

Generic categories 67
Goals 223
Goes-without-saying criteria 89

H

Helper 121
Hero 121
Hierarchy of human needs 118

I

Identify with 110, 191
Identity prism 111
Identity prism model 34
Industry fluidity 28
Influence 30, 40, 190
Innocent 121
Intelligently naïve 77
Internal culture 188

J

Jester 121

L

Lover 121
Loyalty 33

M

Magician 121
Management tool 209
Market communication 28
Marketing mix 33
Market leader 57, 65, 66, 69
Maslow 118
Messaging analysis 100
Metastory 243
Mission 211, 212
Motivation 114, 122

N

Naming 55

O

Organisational change 204
Organisation's culture 214
Overcoming the monster 253

P

Personalities 108
Personality 96, 114, 185
Pioneer 75, 96
Pioneer role 67
Points of differentiation 85
Points of parity 85
Position 65
Positioning 85, 100, 127
Product categories 29
Profiles 189
Protagonist 246
Purchasing decisions 25
Purchasing process 37
Purpose 209

R

Rags to riches 257
Rebel 121
Rebirth 261

Receiver 182
Refection 190
Reference product 52
Relationship 31, 63, 108, 114, 186, 194
Role 30, 63, 65, 79
Ruler 121

S

Sage 121
Sales-triggering 37
Selection choices 83
Selection criteria 56, 66
Self-image 192
Sender 182
Simplified prism 198
Social positioning 40
Story elements 246
Story structure 246
Storytelling 239
Strategic hierarchy 42, 202, 207
Strategic narrative 42, 202, 243
Strategy 39, 202, 227
Strategy map 34
Sub categories 81
Sub category 57, 78
Substitute 78
SWOT 34

T

Testimonies 39
The archetype wheel 121
The cast 247
The Creator 140
The Everyman 121, 144
The Explorer 164
The Helper 132
The Hero 168
The identity prism 179
The Innocent 156
The Jester 148
The Lover 152
The Magician 172
The quest 247, 255
The Rebel 176
The Ruler 136
The Sage 160
The sales funnel 33
The stage 247
Trademarks 108
Tragedy 271
Transaction models 181

U

Unfreeze – change – refreeze 203
Uniformity 110
Unique 95, 186
Unique selling proposition 85
USP (Unique selling point) 33

V

Value chain 67, 207
Value chains 34
Values 41, 115, 188, 214, 247
Verbal identity 188, 238
Vision 211, 232
Visual 189
Visual identity 238
Voyage and return 266

W

Word-of-mouth 37